D1443386

Charlie Chaplin's Own Story

Edited and with an Introduction by

HARRY M. GEDULD

INDIANA UNIVERSITY PRESS / BLOOMINGTON

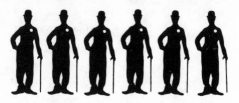

FOR MY DEAR FRIENDS
WAYNE AND MARILYN LEVY
May the Moon always shine as brightly on you as it did on
CHARLIE CHAPLIN

Introduction and notes copyright ©1985 by Harry M. Geduld

Manufactured in the United States of America

Library of Congress Cataloging in Publication Data
Chaplin, Charlie, 1889–1977
Charlie Chaplin's own story.
Bibliography: p.
Includes index.
1. Chaplin, Charlie, 1889–1977. 2. Moving-picture
actors and actresses—United States—Biography.
3. Comedians—United States—Biography. I. Geduld,
Harry M.
PN2287.C5A3   1985   791.43′028′0924 [B]   84-43173
ISBN 0-253-11179-X

1 2 3 4 5   89 88 87 86 85

Contents

INTRODUCTION

THE "LOST" AUTOBIOGRAPHY

When Ellery Sedgwick said that autobiographies ought to begin with chapter two he might almost have been thinking of the special case of Charlie Chaplin. Most of what we know about Chaplin's early life is derived from his autobiographical writings. And that, for the biographer, is where the trouble begins. For Chaplin was a peculiarly unreliable autobiographer.

Over the years Chaplin provided abundant sources of information about his early life: (1) Various articles and interviews scattered through newspapers and periodicals over a fifty-year period, beginning in 1915. Much of this material was ghost-written and has the smell of promotional publicity, but some of it was undoubtedly authentic, and even the ghost-written pieces contain information that must have come from Chaplin himself. (2) *Charlie Chaplin's Own Story* (1916), the comedian's first autobiography which is reprinted here for the first time since its original publication. Original copies of this work are exceedingly rare since most of the edition was destroyed by the publisher (Bobbs-Merrill of Indianapolis) at Chaplin's request. As Raoul Sobel and David Francis note: "To his deep confusion Chaplin had discovered that facts could be checked and that critics could be as scrupulous about them as he was cavalier."[1] (3) *My Trip Abroad* (1922), published in Great Britain as *My Wonderful Visit*. A romantic-nostalgic account of Chaplin's return visit to England (which he had left a decade earlier to find fame and fortune in the United States), the book was co-authored or ghost-written by Monta Bell, a Hollywood screenwriter, producer and director and the "literary editor" of Chaplin's 1923 film, *A Woman of Paris*. (4) *My Autobiography* (1964), Chaplin's official and putatively definitive story of his life and work, which frequently contradicts his earlier auto-biographical writings. Sobel and Francis observe that "since [1916] . . . the world has learned to be very wary of what he has to say about himself, and one might have imagined that having realized this he would have mended his ways. But, alas, when his autobiography appeared in 1964, it merely confirmed the suspicion that he had not changed."[2] (5) *My Life in Pictures* (1975), Chaplin's personal photo-album with his occasional, sometimes idiosyncratic comments on the pictures.

The reader who wades through all this material discovers it to be replete with contradictions and errors, omissions and falsehoods. Chaplin's fondness for spinning colorful tales about his childhood always outweighed his concern for accuracy. Thus his biographers, forced to lean heavily on such question-able material, have frequently been obliged to compromise by recounting what they cannot disprove rather than by narrating what they are able to verify. As Kalton Lahue puts it: "Charles Chaplin and his work have been dissected over and over again, but the interested reader quickly finds himself mired in a quicksand of conflicting opinions, interpretations and even the facts surrounding this comedian's career. When Chaplin an-nounced he was writing his autobiography a few years back, cinema students eagerly awaited what they hoped was to be the definitive explanation from the one man who knew best, only to be bitterly disappointed. Chaplin seemed no better qualified as a source of information about his career and art than the lesser comics who had worked with him, which appears to prove that all had at least two things in common—poor memories and large egos."[3]

At this point the reader may, understandably, question the

need to republish a highly suspect autobiography that was rejected by its author soon after its original appearance. There are, however, as we shall see, a number of good reasons for reissuing it—quite aside from its intrinsic interest as Chapliniana.

To begin with, Chaplin's biographers have often conveyed misleading information about this work. Some state that the Library of Congress owns the only extant copy (although I know of at least three others). Others maintain that *every copy* was destroyed in 1916 (although, curiously enough, Donald W. McCaffrey reprinted several pages of this "lost" autobiography in his 1973 *Focus on Chaplin*). Still others who have no doubts that the work is extant, have dismissed it as a piece of pure fiction without bothering to read it. This reprint removes, at long last, any justification for such false assumptions about the book.

Charlie Chaplin's Own Story (hereafter called *CCOS*) is, in its original form, a volume of 258 pages of large type. It covers a time span that extends from Chaplin's humble and obscure birth in 1889 to the signing of his contract with the Mutual Company in 1916, when he was unquestionably the world's most famous personality and was well on his way to becoming a multimillionaire. This same period is covered in chapters 1–13 of *My Autobiography* (*MA*), but there are significant differences of style and substance between the two works. By contrast with the relatively limpid style of *MA, CCOS* reads like a deliberate imitation of Dickens. This characteristic was probably injected into the "narrative" by Mrs. Rose Wilder Lane, a novelist whom Chaplin thanked for her "invaluable editorial assistance" in a note on the verso of the book's title-page. Almost everyone who has commented on *CCOS* has assumed from this that the autobiography was ghost-written by Mrs. Lane, and this has often been cited as a reason for rejecting the work as inauthentic.

Quite inconsistently, the same scholars who use this argument to ignore *CCOS* feel no compunction about drawing upon other ghost-written autobiographies (e.g., Mack Sennett's *King of Comedy*) as significant source material. Yet comparison of *CCOS* with *MA* reveals that there is information in the former that Mrs. Lane could only have received from Chaplin—if indeed she was the book's ghost-writer. One of the few biographers who has not hastened to reject *CCOS* while accepting the probability that Mrs. Lane was its author, is John McCabe who comments with rare perception: ". . . at times the book is certainly accurate in spirit if not in detail . . . ."[4] Observing that some of *CCOS* is "melodramatic fiction,"[5] McCabe nevertheless admits to having made "very judicious use" of it in his Chaplin biography. The majority of biographers, who have steered clear of it on the grounds that it is impossible to distinguish its facts from its fiction, seem blissfully unconcerned that this argument is equally applicable to much of the first thirteen chapters of *MA*, which have become widely accepted as the only authoritative source of information on Chaplin's early life. As far as that period is concerned, these two autobiographies are equally fascinating, equally dubious, and strikingly different.

In content, these differences may be briefly summarized as follows: (1) *CCOS* and *MA* provide conflicting versions of the same experiences; (2) each work also deals with experiences that do not figure in the other; (3) *CCOS* mentions details whose inaccuracy can be proven (e.g., Chaplin's claim to have been born in Fontainebleau), while in *MA* Chaplin covered his tracks more subtly by obscuring or ignoring facts that made him uneasy (e.g., the existence of his half-brother, Wheeler Dryden). Having stated these differences, it must be added that any attempt to verify or discredit one or other of these autobiographies is bound to be a largely futile activity. For better or worse (and there is little doubt which it is), nearly all that we know about Chaplin's early life is what he wanted us to know about it. Thus it makes more sense to consider these works not as unreliable autobiographies but as personal "myths" deliberately concocted to provide off-screen counterparts to his on-screen images. In essence, *CCOS* depicts Chaplin as he wished his public to see him in 1916, while *MA* depicts him, with variations, as he wished to bow out on a different public half a century later. Neither depiction is ever seriously inconsistent with the Tramp's many incarnations, but that in *MA* generally seems more plausible because its author was far more guarded—aware that his self-dramatization would make its impact on readers who knew considerably more about him than they had fifty years earlier.

In *Limelight* Calvero (Chaplin) tells Terry (Claire Bloom) that her misfortunes sound like a cheap novelette. In fairness, this same criticism may be levelled at many pages of *CCOS*. Yet for all its naiveties and its pseudo-Dickensian flavor it offers us many unique glimpses into Chaplin's childhood. If, with caution, we choose to regard some of those glimpses as fact, they can be read as a complement to Chaplin's later autobiography. If, on the other hand, we view them as pure fiction, they are no less significant, for, like Chaplin's films we must regard them as the fantasies of a great artist—self-imagings that were more meaningful to their creator than the humdrum reality. As such, *CCOS*, whose import has been lost on virtually every biographer, must await the insights of the psychoanalyst.

CHAPLIN IN THE THEATER

Before his start in the movies in 1914, Chaplin had become a star of the British music hall and was on the way to achieving stardom in American vaudeville. His theatrical career is the one aspect of his early life for which we are not almost totally dependent on his own reminiscences. Much of what he tells us on this subject can, in fact, be verified, discredited, or augmented by various other sources, including playbills, press reviews, and the recollections of other performers who observed or worked with him during this period. It is unlikely that we shall ever know the entire story of Chaplin's fifteen years in the music hall and vaudeville, but the detailed account that follows should provide the reader with a documented supplement to *Charlie Chaplin's Own Story* and *My Autobiography*.

Both of these works indicate that Chaplin began his theatrical career as a clog dancer in a juvenile troupe. Clog dancing originated in Lancashire in the 1870s and became a popular British folk art by the end of the nineteenth century. It was a form of step dance in which the heels and toes beat out rapid and complex rhythms. The most difficult steps, known as "nerve dancing," could be performed only by the most experienced and talented dancers. The clogs used were not the quaint all-wooden Dutch variety but were made of more mundane leather uppers with wooden soles and wooden heels equipped with metal studs or tips. Because they were usually worn by impoverished laborers who could not afford all-leather boots and shoes, clogs ordinarily symbolized a back-breaking life of toil and poverty. By contrast, clog *dancing* was a triumphant denial of the plodding, soul-destroying misery that the clogs themselves represented. Hindsight suggests that a form of dancing which expressed the triumph of agility and exuberance over hardship and adversity was a perfectly appropriate activity for the future Tramp.

The two autobiographies offer entirely different accounts of Charlie's career as a clog dancer. *CCOS* is a tale of misfortune with a distinctly Dickensian flavor, but *MA* tells a more restrained and more credible story. According to the later account, Charlie, aged eight, knew nothing whatever about clog dancing, but he often pirouetted for pennies to the strains of a barrel organ. By chance, one of his impromptu performances was seen by John Willie Jackson, manager of the Eight Lancashire Lads, who was impressed by what he saw but at that time had no need of Charlie's talents. However, when one of the Lads in Jackson's troupe became seriously ill, Mr. Holden, manager of the Canterbury Theatre, remembered that his old acquaintance, Charles Chaplin Sr., had a young son who loved to dance. Jackson recognized the boy instantly and he needed no further recommendation. And so, with his parents' permission, Charlie became the youngest member of the eight Lancashire Lads.

During the Christmas season of 1897 the troupe made a big hit when they appeared as a supporting act in Walter Reynolds' pantomime *Babes in the Wood*, starring Edith St. Clair and Lily Austin, at the Leeds Theatre Royal. For nearly two years thereafter they were in constant demand all over the Midlands and North of England. Among the many houses at which the Lads played during their northern circuit were the Sunderland Palace, the Newcastle Empire, and the Star Palace in Barrow. More than half a century later Chaplin still remembered the Newcastle engagement "because on the same bill was a Russian giant who was unable to be accommodated at any of the usual theatrical apartments in the city and the stage manager had solved the problem by constructing a make-shift bed in the theatre's property room which the giant occupied during his stay."[6]

Young Charlie's experience with the troupe gradually convinced him that there was no future in being a mere clog dancer. "I was ambitious to do a single act," he tells us in *MA*, "not only because it meant more money but because I instinctively felt it to be more gratifying than just dancing. I would have liked to be a boy comedian—but that would have required nerve, to stand on the stage alone. Nevertheless, my first impulse to do something other than dance was to be funny. My ideal was a double act, two boys dressed as comedy tramps . . . but, alas, it never materialized."[7] His one chance at a solo performance occurred when Jackson discovered him entertaining the rest of the troupe with an imitation of Bransby Williams interpreting various Dickens characters. The impersonations excited Jackson so much that he talked the manager of a theater in Middlesborough into letting Charlie try them out on a live audience. When the great moment arrived, the prodigy hobbled on stage disguised as an old man. That brought a few laughs, but the rest of the act was unmitigated disaster. He was paralyzed with stage fright. When he opened his mouth nothing came out but an inaudible whisper. The curtain was lowered precipitously and Charlie was dragged offstage. From then on until the end of the tour, Jackson confined him to clog dancing.[8]

Despite this early setback, Chaplin was beginning his real apprenticeship as a professional entertainer. As he toured the variety halls, all that his parents had taught him from their own theatrical experience was being augmented by close observation of the talents of such artists as Marie Lloyd, Harry Champion, Gus Elen, and above all the marvelous Dan Leno. The world of British music hall, then passing through its golden age, became his private academy of comedic arts.

In *MA* Chaplin tells us that as a boy he admired most of all those acts that exploited agility and physical dexterity. He spent long hours studying the performances of Zarmo "the comedy tramp juggler." Curiously, it was the juggling not the tramp character that interested him. He discovered how intense discipline enabled Zarmo to achieve incredible feats of legerdemain that seemed quite simple on stage. It took days of practice with tin plates and rubber balls to convince young Charlie that he

would never pose a serious challenge to the comedy tramp juggler. He turned his attention next to the art of aerobatics, but
when he slipped and sprained a thumb trying to turn a double
somersault, his dream of glory on the high wire came to an
even more abrupt end than did that of the tramp-hero of his
future film, *The Circus*.

It is impossible to determine with certainty which of the
great music-hall comedians influenced Chaplin the most. *MA*
admits, ungenerously, to no particular indebtedness. Yet others
have noticed more than a coincidental similarity between the
artistry of Chaplin and that of Dan Leno (1860-1904).[9] Chaplin states that he never saw Leno in his prime and then
brushes him aside as "more of a character actor than a comedian."[10] But Harold Scott speaks for many aficionados of the
music hall who found it impossible to avoid the association of
Charlie Chaplin with Dan Leno. "It is," Scott insists, "both a
physical and psychological resemblance. Their traditions and
early environment are of the same kind: both found their
education for the stage in the London streets and their technique was grounded in their experience of the cheapest and
rowdiest of music-halls."[11] Onstage Leno often wore an old fe-
dora over his straggly hair, a carelessly tied cravat, absurdly elongated boots, a baggy jacket and oversized pants that flapped
loosely around his frail body. "He had frighteningly large
eyes . . . and high arched eyebrows set in a perpetual expression of surprise. His face was emaciated, and as though to make
himself look even more emaciated, he usually painted two black
lines stretching from the bridge of his nose to his forehead."[12]
That haunting face was capable of an amazing range of con-
tortions. When he laughed he would bend his back and clasp
his hands below his waist; his eyes would close to narrow slits
and his wide mouth would open cavernously in a grotesque
grimace that could suggest an inconsolable anguish almost as

much as it (more often) conveyed his unrestrained hilarity. Leno's forte was comic songs and cockney characterizations touched with pathos. He would "run upon the stage in a series of funny little jerks . . . slap down a comically shod foot"[13] and launch into a long monologue—usually in the role of a familiar working-class type: a washerwoman, a widow, a racing tout. "His material was the sum of all the small things in the life of his class. It was full of babies' bottles, Sunday clothes, pawnshops, lodgings, cheap holidays and the like."[14]

Like Chaplin, Leno began his career as a clog dancer. Slightly shorter than Charlie, he was far more agile, a bundle of nervous energy on india-rubber legs. It is said that he could leap six feet backwards and land on tiptoe! In the 1880s, in Lancashire, the home of clog dancing, he was acclaimed world's champion clog dancer. Ernest Short remarks: "In Lancashire in the 'eighties, clog-dancing was not a mug's game. . . . [The] audience knew the finer points of the art almost as well as the judges. . . . Dan could dance for twenty minutes without an error and yet include original steps in his display."[15]

When it came to clog dancing, Chaplin was never in Leno's class. If he ever gave an outstanding performance it was probably in the last show that his father saw. A theatrical benefit had been arranged on behalf of Chaplin Sr. and the Eight Lancashire Lads were invited to participate. As Charlie recalls it: "The night of the benefit my father appeared on the stage breathing with difficulty, and with a painful effort made a speech. I stood at the side of the stage watching him, not realizing that he was a dying man."[16]

Charlie's days with the Lancashire Lads were also numbered. He was looking pale and drawn and his mother came to the conclusion that he had contracted tuberculosis. She accused Jackson of having overworked her son and destroyed his health. Not unexpectedly, Jackson dismissed the boy from

the troupe. Charlie was indeed getting sick. It was not tuberculosis, however, but a severe case of asthma that was to hang
on for several months.

When he recovered, Charlie decided that it was time for
him to resume his contributions to the family income. In rapid
succession he tried his hand as an errand boy in a chandler's
shop, a receptionist for a firm of insurance doctors, a page boy
to a wealthy family in Lancaster Gate, an assistant in one of
W. H. Smith's stationery stores, a learner-laborer at a glass-
blowing factory, and a Wharfdale operator in Straker's
printing-house. None of these jobs netted him more than
twelve shillings a week and he was fired from several of them
because he was too puny to manage the work.

According to some accounts he continued his theatrical
career at the age of ten in a production of H. Chance Newton's
Giddy Ostend; or the Absent-Minded Millionaire, which was presented at the London Hippodrome beginning on January 6,
1900. The show was advertised as a "Grand Spectacular Aqua-
tic Carnival" with music by George Jacobi. It starred Little
Tich, James Finney, Elsie Carew, and Fritz Rimma. Nothing is
known about Charlie's part in the production but it must have
been quite insignificant as his name is not mentioned in either
the cast-list or reviews. Also in 1900, according to Sobel and
Francis,[17] but two years later according to *CCOS,* the future
comedian played a street waif in a provincial production of
Charles A. Taylor's *From Rags to Riches.* I have tried and failed,
to turn up any reliable information on this presentation, and
find Chaplin's own detailed but novelettish account of it ex-
tremely dubious.

Again at the London Hippodrome, starting on Boxing Day
(December 16) 1900, Charlie played the rather prominent role
of the kitchen cat in W. H. Risquer's pantomime of *Cinderella,*
for which Jacobi again supplied the music. This was a truly lav-

ish production. Amy Farrell appeared as Cinderella along with Windham Guise as the Baron de Vere, Hetty Chattell as the Prince, Ruth Lytton as Dandini, and Marceline, the great French clown, as Buttons. This stellar cast was supported by such vaudeville acts as the Trentanovi Sisters (athletic trapeze artists), the Great Schaeffer Family (equestrians), Inaudi the Human Phonograph, Leon Morris's Educated Ponies, and Captain Woodward's Performing Seals, as well as by a Comic Water Pantomime and a display of Electrical Fairy Fountains. Despite the spectacle, the greatest audience response was reserved for little Charlie. In one scene of the *Cinderella* story, Marceline edged away from a snarling "dog" and deliberately fell over Charlie the cat. The clown's pratfall got some laughs but they were nothing compared to the roars of laughter that Charlie received when he suddenly arched his back, sniffed at the dog's rear end, winked at the audience, and then suggestively cocked his leg against the scenery.[18]

MA mentions neither *Giddy Ostend* nor *From Rags to riches*, and it assigns the *Cinderella* episode to the period when Charlie was still touring with the Lads. Instead of these productions, Chaplin refers to the role of Sammy the Newsboy in H. A. Saintsbury's *Jim: A Romance of Cockayne* as his first theatrical venture after leaving Jackson's troupe. In a *Photoplay* interview of 1915, he had declared that this play was "the first show I have any very definite recollection of [acting in]." In *MA*, he maintains that he was twelve and a half—and that would have been in October or November 1901; but the play was actually reviewed in July 1903 when he was fourteen.

Mr. Blackmore, his theatrical agent, gave him a note to C. E. Hamilton at Charles Frohman's office. There he was offered the interim role of Sammy the Newsboy to be followed by a forty weeks' tour as Billy the Pageboy in William Gillette's play, *Sherlock Holmes*. The salary was two pounds ten shillings per week—take it or leave it. Charlie took it.[19]

Jim was a melodrama about Roydon Carstairs (H. A. Saintsbury), a young nobleman sometimes called "The Dook," who, in the second of the play's four acts shares a garret with Sammy, a Cockney urchin, and "Jim," a beautiful, incurably sick flower girl (Dorothea Desmond) who was almost certainly Chaplin's original inspiration for the heroine of *City Lights*. The police suspect Carstairs of having murdered James Gatlock, husband of Alma Traherne whom "The Dook" had once loved. "Jim" altruistically exonerates Carstairs by implicating herself, but evidence is produced to prove that she was sick in bed when the murder took place. In the final act, Alma discovers that "Jim" is the long-lost daughter she had abandoned seventeen years earlier. Stricken with remorse, she confesses to the murder of her husband and then takes her own life.

In *MA* Chaplin tells us that his role in *Jim* was "a big part, about thirty-five sides." This sounds like exaggeration since Sammy's importance was largely confined to the second act, but there is no available playscript to verify this one way or the other. At this period, as a result of his erratic education, reading was a problem for Charlie—so his older brother Sydney had to read his lines to him. He memorized them in three days and then turned up for rehearsals in the upstairs foyer of the Drury Lane Theatre. "Those rehearsals," he tells us, "were a revelation. They opened up a new world of technique. I had no idea that there was such a thing as stagecraft—timing, pausing, a cue to turn, to sit—but it came naturally to me. Only one fault Mr. Saintsbury corrected: I moved my head and mugged too much when I talked."[20]

Unfortunately, Saintsbury's elaborate rehearsals could not save the play. The melodrama bombed. Beginning July 6,

1903, a week's tryout at the Royal Court Theatre, Kingston-on-Thames, was followed by a week at the Fulham Grand. The critics turned thumbs down on the play and it folded forever after the last night (July 18) in Fulham. Nevertheless, Charlie received what were probably his first notices. *The Era* appraised his performance on two separate occasions. While the play was still running at Kingston-on-Thames, *The Era* reviewer commented: "Of the others taking part in the play mention should be made of . . . Master Charles Chaplin, who, as a newsboy known as Sam, showed promise." After the Fulham opening, the same paper rhapsodized thus: "Master Charles Chaplin is a broth of a boy as Sam, the newspaper boy, giving a most realistic picture of the cheeky, honest, loyal, self-reliant, philosophic street Arab who haunts the regions of Cockayne."[21] Chaplin himself quotes the following review from the *London Topical Times*:

> . . . there is one redeeming feature, the part of Sammy, a newspaper boy, a smart London street Arab, much responsible for the comic part. Although hackneyed and old-fashioned, Sammy was made vastly amusing by Master Charles Chaplin, a bright and vigorous child actor. I have never heard of the boy before, but I hope to hear great things of him in the near future.[22]

That anonymous reviewer did not have long to wait. Rehearsals for *Sherlock Holmes* got under way as soon as the lights faded out on *Jim*. Saintsbury hoped to recoup all that he had lost on the latter production by reviving the play in which William Gillette had triumphed two years earlier. In that original presentation (September 1901 at the Lyceum Theatre, London), Gillette himself had played Holmes and Henry McArdle was cast as Billy the quick-witted pageboy. In the revival, Saintsbury played the great detective and assigned to Charlie the role that McArdle had first created. As before, brother Sydney helped Charlie master his lines (there were only about forty of them) which were all confined to act two of the four-act drama. Once again, as with *Jim*, Charlie was required to speak in a Cockney accent, addressing Holmes with such lines as "You didn't 'ave nothink, sir."

The revival of *Sherlock Holmes* opened at the Pavilion Theatre, London, on July 27, 1903, and the new Billy was soon earning critical plaudits. "The part," commented *The Era*, ". . . is well played by Mr. Charles Chaplin, who succeeds in making the smart pageboy a prime favorite with the audience."[23]

Saintsbury's *Sherlock Holmes* was a huge success. It toured England and Wales, playing to packed houses for forty weeks; it was held over in the London suburbs for another two months and then embarked on a second tour only three weeks after completing the first. At Christmas 1903, at Charlie's request, his brother Sydney was brought into the show when it reached the Theatre Royal, Dewsbury. He was given the role of the Count Von Stahlburg. This was the first time the two brothers had ever appeared on stage together.[24]

At the start of 1905, Kenneth Rivington, Saintsbury's Dr. Watson, took *Sherlock Holmes* on a new tour. This time Rivington played Holmes. Charlie continued in the role of Billy. This tour ended in April. Then, in May 1905, Harry Yorke, proprietor of Blackburn's Theatre Royal, acquired the rights to present Gillette's play on the small-town circuit. Charlie was kept on in the role of Billy, and as the only remaining member of the Saintsbury revival, he was treated by the new director as an authority on all aspects of the production. He became, in effect, the play's assistant producer. But the cockiness with which this sixteen-year-old trouper proffered his suggestions did not endear him to the rest of the cast. Everyone was delighted when he quit the show on September 25 after receiving a telegram from William Postance,[25] Gillette's stage manager, offering him a part in a curtain-raiser.

William Gillette had recently arrived in London from his native America to co-star with Lucille La Verne and Marie Doro in his new comedy, *Clarice*. His *Sherlock Holmes* had been a triumph on both sides of the Atlantic, but the British critics gave the new play an unmerciful pasting. Some of them even stooped to making cheap jibes at the actor's American accent. Gillette struck back with *The Painful Predicament of Sherlock Holmes* subtitled "A Fantasy—in about One-Tenth of an Act." This brief skit, curiously reminiscent of Strindberg's *The Stronger*, contained three main characters but only two speaking roles. In response to his critics, Gillette who played Holmes of course, sat onstage without uttering a word throughout the entire piece. As the curtain went up Billy (Chaplin) could be heard offstage remonstrating with Gwendolyn Cobb (Irene Vanbrugh), a young woman who is trying to force her way into the great detective's study. Billy shuts the door in her face and turns to speak to Holmes:

> "I beg your pardon, sir—If you please, sir!—It's a young lady 'as just come in, an' says she must see you—she's 'ere now, sir, a-tryin' to pull the door open—but I don't like 'er eye, sir! . . . I don't like it at all, sir! 'Er eye is certainly bad, sir! An' she—don't seem to be able to leave off talkin' long enough fer me to tell 'er as 'ow she can't see you, sir! I tried to tell 'er as you give orders not to see no one. I shouted it out tremendous—but she was talkin' so loud it never got to 'er—so I run up to warn you—an' she come runnin' after me—an'—an'—An' . . . an' 'ere she is, sir!"

Gwendolyn thereupon bursts into the room "with unrestricted enthusiasm." She takes over Holmes's study, steps on his treasured violin, removes his favorite pictures from the wall and treats him to a twenty-minute monologue on the sad fate of her lover—the moneylender Levi Lichtenstein—who has been thrown into jail by her ruthless father. At a signal from Holmes, Billy exits. Gwendolyn's harangue is turning into a fit of hysterics when Billy re-enters with two uniformed men who promptly drag her offstage. As the curtain falls, Billy turns to Holmes and tacitly comments: "It was the *right* asylum, sir," while the master-sleuth injects a shot of morphia into his arm and falls languidly back onto a pile of cushions.

In describing this skit, Chaplin makes no mention of the bitter irony of his having had to cope with a real-life mad-woman—his own mother—only a few years earlier.[26] He preferred to recall his first glimpse of the exquisite Marie Doro with whom he fell instantly and hopelessly in love. He worshipped her discreetly—from the wings—throughout every performance of *Clarice*.

Not even Marie's luminous beauty could save Gillette's comedy, and *The Painful Predicament*, which had premiered on October 3, 1905, folded along with *Clarice* on October 14 after a mere dozen performances. Following Saintsbury's example, Gillette, to recoup his losses, within three days mounted yet another revival of *Sherlock Holmes*—also at the Duke of York's—taking the star role for himself and reassigning to Kenneth Rivington the part of Dr. Watson. Alice Faulkner, the heroine, was played by Marie Doro—a fact that delighted Charlie until he discovered that none of his scenes coincided with hers. His disappointment was tempered, however, by the pride and pleasure of appearing nightly before a distinguished and enthusiastic audience. Every celebrity in London seemed to be flocking to see the production. The company performed before various members of the British royal family as well as the King of Greece and Prince Christian of Denmark, and Charlie was greeted by novelist Hall Caine, playwright Dion Boucicault, and Lord Kitchener of Khartoum when they came backstairs to shake hands with Gillette. He rubbed shoulders with even more notables when the company attended the funeral of Sir Henry Irving at Westminster Abbey. During the service he knelt in solemn prayer between Lewis Waller, London's dashing matinée idol, and "Dr." Walford Bodie "of bloodless surgery fame" whom he would soon burlesque in *Casey's Circus*.

After the completion of the London run of *Sherlock Holmes* (the last night was in December 1905), Charlie continued with the production during a short provincial tour (January 1–March 5, 1906). Right throught to the last night he confidently expected that the show would cross the Atlantic as soon as the British run had ended. But his expectations were dashed when the final curtain descended and Gillette bade farewell to the cast. Instead of a ticket to New York, he handed his "Billy" a letter of recommendation to Madge Kendal. On the strength of this letter Mrs. Kendal was prepared to offer him a place in her company. It was a fine opportunity, but Charlie flatly rejected it when he heard that it meant going on another provincial tour. After treading the boards with the great William Gillette he would consider nothing less than an important West End engagement. As a result of his snobbish obstinacy he was never again to appear in a play, and two long months were to pass before he found regular work in the theater. By that time he was ready to accept any opening that came his way.

His less fastidious brother Sydney was seldom out of a job for very long. As soon as his short run with *Sherlock Holmes* had ended, he joined Charlie Manon's comedians, a troupe that specialized in performing slapstick and pantomime sketches to the strains of ballet music. It was not long before his talents came to the attention of Fred Karno who lured him away from Manon with a salary offer of four pounds a week. Sydney was now a member of Britain's foremost company of pantomime-comedians.

INTRODUCTION

While Sydney toured with one of Karno's provincial troupes, his younger brother remained in London frittering away his money. "Whores, sluts and an occasional drinking bout weaved in and out of this period," Chaplin tells us, "but neither wine, women nor song held my interest for long. I really wanted romance and adventure."[27] The theater held out a promise of both — if only he could find his way back into the big time. Hopefully, he announced his availability in the "Professional Cards" columns of *The Stage*:

> Master Charles Chaplin
>   *Sherlock Holmes* Co.
> Disengaged March 5th [1906].
> Coms. 9 Tavistock Place. Tele., 2, 187 Hop.[28]

There was no response.

Then Sydney came to rescue by negotiating the first of many contracts for his kid brother. Charlie, who had just turned seventeen, had to pocket his pride, for he was to get no separate billing and the job was a definite comedown as far as he was concerned. "I who had been a hit in a West End theater [to be] acting [in] a low vulgar comedy in dirty fourth-rate houses. . . .Then . . . at last, persuaded by the offer of a pound a week and a long engagement, I consented to become a member of *Casey's Circus*."[29]

The actual contract reveals that Charlie did rather better financially than he remembered:

> May 26, 1906
>
> I, the guardian of Charles Chaplin, agree for him to appear in *Casey's Court* [sic] wherever it may be booked in the British Isles only, the agreement to commence May 14, 1906, at a salary weekly of £2 5s. (two pounds five shillings), increase [sic] to £2 10s, the week commencing July 1906.
> All travelling expenses paid by Mr. Harry Cardle.

INTRODUCTION

The said Charles Chaplin to assist in anything connected with the performance that may be a reasonable request.

Should the said Charles Chaplin do anything of an exceptional nature, that is likely to bring scandal on the management dismissal without notice.

To terminate this contract, two weeks' notice must be given on either side.

In the event of a week out, board and residence only will be paid, but no salary.

SYDNEY CHAPLIN
ERNEST CARDLE
HARRY CARDLE.[30]

The Era described *Casey's Court* as a "turn full of animation, illustrating court [i.e. alley] life among the poor. Thirty smart juveniles sing, act, dance, and make merry in rousing style."[31] Their merriment consisted mainly in wearing clothes that were many sizes too big for them and burlesquing the pompous behavior of adults. (They would have reminded Americans of the period of the antics of the slum characters in R. F. Outcault's pioneer comic strip, *The Yellow Kid.*) The show was so popular that the Cardles spun off a sequel entitled *Casey's Circus.* Contrary to what the contract indicates, Charlie was assigned to the sequel and not to *Casey's Court.* He remained with it throughout a long tour, from its premier at the Bradford Empire on May 14, 1906 until the show closed at Sadler's Wells, London, on July 20, 1907.

From the outset he considered that his worst fears about the show were amply justified. *Casey's Circus* was deplorably lowbrow stuff: its general level of comedy never rose above crude caricature. To be dragged down to it would be disastrous for his reputation. He had to find some way to transform his roles, to make them more striking, more memorable than anyone else's. He had parts in two sketches—a travesty of Dick Turpin's Ride to York and a parody of "Dr." Walford Bodie, the celebrated huckster who claimed to be able to cure cripples through his unique powers of animal magnetism.[32] Charlie's role in the first sketch was a minor one, but in the second he was cast as "Dr. Body," the "bloodless surgeon" himself, and the temptation to try something original with it proved irresistible. He decided to change it from a mere caricature into a full-blooded character study. He began by studying Bodie at work, keenly observing various details of his dress and deportment, and noting each and every idiosyncratic gesture and movement. Then he spent hours before a mirror painstakingly developing his incarnation of the "miracle doctor." Finally, on opening night he discarded the stock burlesque makeup he was supposed to wear and carefully made himself up to look as much like "Dr." Bodie as possible.

Chaplin's own account of the performance makes it clear that his "Dr." Bodie was shaped by a carefully preconceived theory of comedic character. Norman Mailer has remarked that a great actor playing a drunkard does not try to convey the impression that he is inebriated. He attempts, instead, to project the impression of a man who *believes* that he is sober but behaves like a drunkard in spite of himself. Almost from the outset, Chaplin seems to have discerned the basis of comedy—or at least *his* kind of comedy—in this same notion. In *CCOS* he tells us: "I had stumbled on the secret of being funny—unexpectedly. An idea going in one direction meets an opposite idea suddenly. 'Ha! Ha!' you shriek. It works every time."[33] As far as the characterization of "Dr." Bodie was concerned this meant conveying the impression that he was in absolute earnest though he was behaving in a ludicrous manner. The characterization was an instant success. It made him the star of the show, and he lost no time in asking for—and promptly received—a tidy salary increase for the remainder of the show's run.

INTRODUCTION

Casey's Army, the Cardles' new show, took to the road on July 22, 1907, but Charlie was no longer with the company. The reasons are obscure. Perhaps he was determined to make one more stab at the "legit." Perhaps he had made more salary demands which the Cardles considered exorbitant. At any rate, he was out of work for several months. He tried to make a comeback with a solo act, "Sam Cohen: the Jewish Comedian." This was evidently a rather crude anti-semitic caricature which he had the temerity to try out on a predominantly Jewish audience at Forester's Music Hall in London's East End. He was lucky to escape in one piece. Then he joined a short-lived troupe called The Ten Looneys and played the juvenile lead in *The Merry Major*, a "cheap, depressing" sketch that folded after only a week. He even tried his hand at writing: the result was *Twelve Just Men* (Edgar Wallace's *The Four Just Men* had been published a year or so earlier), a slapstick comedy full of stock theatrical types about a breach of promise case. He sold it to a rascally vaudeville actor who insisted that Charlie direct it as part of the deal and then pulled out of the arrangement as soon as rehearsals got under way.

His outlook began to brighten at last when Sydney got him an appointment with his boss, Fred Karno. According to Karno's biographers, Sydney "used to whisper wheedling words into the Guv'nor's' ear, whenever he got a chance, about the superlative merits of his younger brother."[34] Charlie was ushered into the presence of the king of mime. It wasn't much of an interview. Karno, a short, chunky man with bright eyes, sized up Sydney's brother with the eye of an expert. Whatever else he was capable of, that wan, slightly built youth who stood before him looked physically ill-equipped to withstand the rigors of a slapstick pantomime troupe. However, probably as a gesture to Sydney, one of his rising stars, Karno agreed to employ Charlie as a supernumerary on the understanding that he would be considered for a permanent place in one of the troupes whenever a vacancy arose. It was worth being patient, for when and if he got his opportunity he would be earning a regular salary for fifty-two weeks of the year! And apart from the security, there was also the consideration that working for Karno meant something far superior to the usual run-of-the-mill variety act. Admittedly, it was not as prestigious as acting with William Gillette, but as far as pantomime comedy was concerned, the Karno Company was the tops.

Karno's name was originally Frederick Westcott. Born in Exeter in 1866, before going on the stage he worked as a lace-maker, a barber's assistant, a costermonger, a bricklayer, and a plumber. Then, having trained himself to be a champion gymnast, he began to tour the halls as an acrobat. By the turn of the century he had evolved his first slapstick sketch, *Hilarity*. This was followed in 1901 by *Jail Birds* which featured a comic policeman a dozen years before Mack Sennett launched the Keystone Kops. Thereafter, Karno settled at 26, 28, and 28a Vaughan Road, Camberwell, London, S.E., dubbed "The Fun Factory," where, with the cooperation of Frank Dix and Harold Gatty, he developed a series of slapstick-mime sketches that were to send several generations of music-hall audiences rolling in the aisles. By the time Sydney Chaplin joined Karno, the enterprising Fred had no less than eight companies touring England and the United States with such entertainments as *Early Birds, The Thirsty First, Moses & Son, The Washerwoman*, and, most popular of all, *Mumming Birds*. This last sketch starred three of Karno's best-loved comics, Billy Reeves (who played a much harassed conjurer[35]), Billie Ritchie (the drunken swell), and Charley Bell (the bad lad in the theater-box). A foretaste of Karno's *A Night in an English Music Hall* in which Charlie would play the star role, *Mumming Birds* created its comedy out of the wordless badgering of a serious-minded performer by a mischievous adolescent and an indefatigable drunkard.[36]

Charlie's "big break" with the Karno Company came on September 14, 1907, when he was assigned to play the minor role of an old clothes vendor in the sketch, *London Suburbia*. Karno watched his performance closely, liked what he saw, and offered him the more substantial role of the villain in *The Football Match*. This sketch was presented at the London Coliseum on February 3, 1908, and Charlie was so well-received that Karno gave him a year's contract at four pounds a week.

The Football Match was the most spectacular of Karno's productions. Much of the action took place against an elaborate painted backdrop depicting a crowd of cheering football fans. The absurdly melodramatic plot unfolded in the midst of a Cup Final game played by ex-professional footballers. Charlie entered dressed in a flowing cape, frock coat, top hat and spats, and sporting a drooping moustache beneath a bulbous red nose. His twirling cane was soon discovered (like Dr. Body's) to have a will of its own. As its owner progressed across the stage, the cane persisted in tripping him up or bouncing off props and scenery and striking him on the head. At the same time, his pants, exceptionally obedient to the law of gravity, always seemed to be precariously on the verge of slithering to the ground. Without uttering a word, Charlie established himself as a dandified evil-doer who reduced himself to absurdity with every step he took. The character was, in certain respects, an anticipation of the frenetic, frock-coated villain he was to play in his first film, *Making a Living* (1914). As the sketch unfolded, Charlie sidled up to Stiffy the Goalkeeper—played by Harry Weldon, the star of the show—and tried to bribe him to throw the match. Harry Weldon kept the audience mildly amused with his characteristic grimaces, gurgles, and whistles, but laughter rocked the house whenever the villain indulged in a new bit of comic business. There could be no doubt that the comedy laurels belonged to Chaplin. When he also started to receive better notices than the star of the show, Weldon lost his temper and struck Charlie across the cheek.

Weldon's fit of pique had no influence on Karno—for the "Guv'nor" already regarded Chaplin as a rising talent. Buoyantly, the Chaplin brothers pooled their income, moved into a comfortable apartment at 15 Glenshaw Mansions in the Brixton Road, and hired a maid to handle the housework. Fourteen years later, Charlie rhapsodized about the "nouveau riche" splendors of that bachelor flat; "Glenshore [sic] Mansions—a more prosperous neighborhood. Glenshore Mansions, which meant a step upward to me, where I had my Turkish carpets and my red lights in the beginning of my prosperity."[37]

At nineteen, Chaplin was caught up in an intensely busy schedule of work. He would perform every evening at three different music halls, travelling from one to the other by private bus. Then he would return to Glenshaw Mansions and rehearse until two or three in the morning. Even at this period in his life he was already a tireless perfectionist.

In June 1908 Karno sent him to Paris to appear as the drunken dude in *Mumming Birds* at the Folies Bergère. It was his first trip abroad and he found Paris as exhilarating and enchanting as he had expected. He took a room in the Rue Geoffroy-Marie and set out to sample the culture and decadence of the City of Lights. He whirled through a kaleidoscope of experiences—sampling museums and art galleries, bistros and brothels. He picked a quarrel with a boxer ("I have never fought anyone since") and shrugged off the chance of an introduction to Debussy with the comment, "Never heard of him!"

Back in England he was offered the role of Stiffy the Goalkeeper in a revival of *The Football Match*. Stepping into Harry

Weldon's shoes signified the possibility of stardom and he leapt at the opportunity. But a week into the run he was taken ill and the show closed before the majority of London's theatergoers had a chance to discover him.

Karno next assigned him to his second-string company which toured the Moss and Stoll circuits (a chain of Empire Theaters from Hackney to Glasgow and from Hull to Dublin) with a choice selection of sketches. Charlie played major parts in *Mumming Birds, The G.P.O., Skating*[38] (which had been devised by Sydney), and *The Yap-Yaps*. From time to time Karno would drop in on a performance. Increasingly impressed with Chaplin, he offered him the title role in *Jimmy the Fearless; or The Boy 'Ero* by Charles Baldwin and F. O'Neill. Charlie perused the piece and decided that it was beneath his dignity. The "Guv'nor" thereupon turned the part over to another aspiring talent, young Stanley Jefferson, the future Stan Laurel, who as yet was unacquainted with Oliver Hardy. Charlie soon realized his mistake. As he watched Stanley's performance it became evident that Jimmy was a character who had fascinating comic possibilities. Aware that he had thrown away the very opportunity he had been waiting for, Charlie contritely turned up at the Fun Factory and begged for a second chance. Fortunately, the "Guv'nor" was never one to stand in the way of true talent. If Charlie had changed his mind, the part was his. So it came about that on April 25, 1910, at the Stratford Empire, Charlie Chaplin at last received star billing as a comedian—in Fred Karno's "latest and greatest feast of fun."

As Jimmy the Fearless, Chaplin was an unqualified success from the first night until the show closed at the Bradford Empire on September 3, 1910. The following notice, titled "A Rising Actor," was typical of the encouraging reviews he began to receive in the theatrical and popular press:

To assume roles made famous by Fred Kitchen is no small task for a stripling of twenty-one, yet Mr. Chas. Chaplin, who has caused so much laughter this week as Jimmy the Fearless, has done so with vast credit to himself. Mr. Chaplin has not been more than three years with Mr. Karno, yet he has played all the principal parts, and he fully realizes the responsibility of following so consummate an artist as Fred Kitchen. He is ambitious and painstaking, and is bound to get on. Young as he is, he has done some good work on the stage, and his entrance alone in *Jimmy the Fearless*, sets the house in a roar and stamps him as a born comedian.[39]

Jimmy the Fearless, a sketch in four scenes, was described by a contemporary reviewer as "an amusing skit on a boy's proclivity for reading 'penny dreadfuls'. Jimmy has a bad dream after a hearty supper, and finds himself wandering in the Wild West in the region of the Rocky Mountains. After some exciting adventures in Deadman's Gulch, and hand-to-hand fighting in the Rockies, he rescues the heroine and returns triumphant. Then he wakes up."[40] The curtain descended on the sight of young Jimmy stretched across his father's knee for a vigorous spanking—his punishment for staying out late with "a bit o' skirt." From this account it appears that Charlie was being cast in a backward-looking role that continued his earlier juvenile characterizations in *Jim* and *Sherlock Holmes*. But the sketch also looked forward, at least in form, to such Chaplin films as *Shoulder Arms* and *Sunnyside*, in which a comic plot unfolds within the framework of a dream; it may well have been the original inspiration for this recurrent plot device in Chaplin's films.

It is difficult to gain any clear impression of what Charlie was like at this crucial episode in his life as he stood simultaneously on the threshold of manhood and on the verge of popular success in the music hall. His own recollections are filtered through a romantic haze, and those biographers who have tried to picture him at this period have often been guided by hind-sight rather than by any special understanding. It is reasonable to surmise, however, that Karno's budding star was a rather different person from the young man who, merely a decade later, would be able to claim without much arrogance or exaggeration, "I am quite well known in Tibetan lamaseries where the name of Jesus Christ has never been heard."[41] In fact, three distinct and more or less incompatible personae emerge from his miscellaneous accounts of his early life. First there was the young rip or 'cut-up,' revelling in every available low-life pleasure. Second was the would-be sophisticate, assuming the dress, deportment, and supercilious attitudes of a particular type of English gentleman. Third was the introvert, spending long hours alone at his violin or poring obsessively over weighty philosophical tomes in a search for the elusive "meaning" of life. Which of these individuals—if any—was the authentic young Charlie Chaplin? It is difficult, if not impossible, to imagine him tugging off his comic red nose and settling down to read Schopenhauer, or setting aside his violin and donning a tuxedo to pay a visit to the local whorehouse. Taken together, the various personae of Chaplin's autobiographical writings give the impression of a collection of masks deliberately worn to conceal an identity that its owner has always been ashamed of or afraid to expose too fully. The image of the young rip looks suspiciously like an attempt to emulate the bon vivant reputation of his father, while the image of the sophisticate appears to be a model of refinement, "the swell" that his mother would have approved of . The third image, that of the introvert, seems to be on a par with Chaplin's fabrication about being born in France[42]—that is, an older man's fantasy recreation of his past to make it appear more 'relevant' or 'suitable' than it really was.

If anyone knew what the young Charlie Chaplin was like it

was his brother Sydney, but unfortunately, from that source there was permanent silence on the subject. Possibly Charlie was not yet quite sure of himself, but in his work he seems to have displayed a mood of self-confidence bordering on cockiness, an attitude that would develop into that extreme egotism that sometimes stunned those who came to know him in Hollywood. The few surviving photographs of the period depict him—offstage—as a smart but sober dresser. One of those pictures shows him sporting a respectable-looking derby hat and a high-starched collar; the tight-lipped expression on his sallow face resolutely concealed the undignified fact that it belonged to one of England's most gifted laughter-makers.[43]

This improbable-looking comedian was certainly not the person that Alf Reeves, manager of Karno's American company, had in mind when he crossed the Atlantic to request the "Guv'nor" to release one of his top-flight comics for a tour of the United States. Reeves desperately needed a replacement for his brother Billy whom Flo Ziegfeld had just lured away from his triumph in the New York production of Karno's *A Night in an English Music Hall* to appear in the first *Ziegfeld Follies*. Alf Reeves expected an "established" name like Harry Weldon or Billie Ritchie, but Karno inexplicably singled out this young upstart Chaplin to take the lead in *The Wow-Wows*, a follow-up to *The Yap-Yaps*.

In its British production *The Wow-Wows* had starred Sydney Chaplin in the part of the Hon. Archibald Binks, the role that his brother would play on Broadway. Charlie was familiar with the sketch and had a low opinion of it, but he was not going to repeat the mistake he had made over *Jimmy the Fearless*. This time he was prepared to overlook the shortcomings of the piece in order to tour the United States as a vaudeville star.

Alf Reeves's reservations about Chaplin were abandoned as soon as he saw him at work, and from that time onwards he

played a major part in furthering the comedian's career. As Denis Gifford notes: "it was . . . Alfred who acted as producer-manager to . . . Chaplin's American tours. And it was Alf Reeves who became Chaplin's own manager in the movies."[44]

Chaplin, unlike Columbus, had to be discovered by America and not vice versa. To accomplish this feat would take more than one visit. The first enabled Charlie to see for himself how the reality of the United States differed from his illusions about it. But, more important, it determined whether he would want to make a second visit. If he had decided that one experience was sufficient, it is unlikely that he would ever have made a movie, for his film career and his meteoric rise to fame were the chance outcome of his second transatlantic tour.

The first visit started out with an unpleasant twelve-day crossing—by cattle-boat—to Quebec. The Karno troupe, numbering fifteen in all, then took the train to New York via Toronto, arriving in Manhattan on a peaceful Sunday morning.[45] Charlie found Times Square "somewhat of a let-down . . . and Broadway looked seedy, like a slovenly woman just out of bed."[46] That first, disillusioning sight of New York was to linger with him. Five years later he told a reporter for *Photoplay*: "I sat looking out of the window of the shabby little boarding house bedroom. The Times Tower loomed in the sky and I sat there with my head on the window sill and cried, I felt so lonely and forlorn. That was the loneliest I have ever been."[47]

He was soon too busy to think about anything but work. Rehearsals got under way, and *The Wow-Wows* and his part in it became all-important. The troupe had a six-week's engagement with the Percy Williams circuit, and their success or failure would turn on their immediate appeal to the tough-minded vaudeville audiences of New York. If they proved popular their

stay in the U.S. would doubtless be extended. If not, another cattle-boat would be waiting to take them back to England.

For the first two weeks *The Wow-Wows* lived up to Charlie's poor opinion of it: at its out-of-town opening it bombed with one audience after another. Apparently they were bewildered or bored by the sketch's rather localized British humor: it focused on the efforts of a group of boys, camping beside the Thames, to teach one of their number a well-deserved "lesson," by giving him a rough-and-tumble initiation into their secret society. Nothing Charlie could do with the sketch seemed to make much difference. In the third week, however, the troupe played the Colonial Theater in Manhattan before a predominantly British audience—mainly servants from the posh residences of Fifth Avenue. Here the show got a rousing reception, and *The Wow-Wows* quickly became the talk of the town. This favorable turn of events was due to the snob appeal of the latest import from England rather than to the talents of Chaplin and his supporting cast. Be that as it may, the troupe began receiving favorable notices and contract offers started to roll in from the various theater circuits. Among the earliest was one in *Variety* that focused on Chaplin:

> Chaplin is typically English, the sort of comedian that the American audiences seem to like, although unaccustomed to. His manner is quiet and easy, and he goes about his work in a devil-may-care manner, in direct contrast to the twenty-minutes-from-a-cemetery makeup he employs. Chaplin will do all right for America.[48]

Pretty soon Alf Reeves had negotiated a contract that gave the company a twenty-weeks' coast-to-coast tour on the Sullivan and Considine circuit. Money-conscious Chaplin was doubtless as elated by the salary he would be getting as he must have felt about the rave reviews, and for the rest of the tour he regularly socked away fifty dollars of his seventy-five-a-week salary.[49]

Beginning March 1911, at the Empress Theater, Chicago, the repertoire of the troupe was augmented by *A Night in an English Music Hall* which rapidly became Chaplin's most popular sketch. As seen by a contemporary reviewer:

> It shows a stage upon a stage with two tiers of boxes, its audience and performers, and gives the conditions of an English variety house some years ago. The principal comedian of the company is the "Souse," who occupies a lower box and who is principal in making things merry until he finishes on the stage himself in a wrestling match with the "terrible Turk" of the show. In this role Charles Chaplin is the equal of Billy Reeves who orginally created the role.[50]

The tour took the troupe through most of the great cities north of the Mason-Dixon Line. A correspondent for the *Vancouver News* described their reception, repeated in theater after theater from coast to coast:

> The Fred Karno Company in *A Night in an English Music Hall* at the Orpheum this week is doing a phenomenal business, and the house is packed for every performance. There are very few people in the city who have not seen this act, and they all enjoy it. Charles Chaplin is deservedly featured.[51]

After playing Los Angeles, the troupe returned to New York where they had a six weeks' engagement for the William Morris Agency, starting in April 1911 at the American Theater on 42nd Street. As the irrepressible drunken dude in *A Night in an English Music Hall* Chaplin was scoring his first unequivocal successes with American audiences, and it was around this time— if his memory served him correctly—that Mack Sennett first saw the comedian who was to become his greatest 'discovery'.

Mabel [Normand] and I saw top-drawer vaudeville at Oscar Hammerstein's Victoria at Seventh Avenue and Forty-Second Street and looked at Mr. Morris's offering as an afterthought. We caught one act called "A Night in a London [sic] Music Hall," which was more hilarious than anything at Hammerstein's. A "little Englisher," as Mabel called him, duded up in a frock coat, played the part of a drunken spectator in a box. He got into the act on stage, of course, and took part in a knockabout comic fight with the other English actors. The most striking effect of his make-up was an enormous red nose.

"Feller's pretty funny," Mabel said.

"Think he'd be good for pictures?" I said.

"He might be," Mabel said. . . .

I leafed through the program and found his name. Chaplin.

"I don't know," I said to Mabel. "He has all the tricks and routines and he can take a fall, and probably do a 108, but that limey make-up and costume—I don't know."

I filed a note to keep this comedian in mind.[52]

Following the William Morris engagement, the troupe took off on yet another Sullivan and Considine tour—an additional twenty weeks on the big-city circuit. It took them as far west as San Francisco (June 1911). Then they returned to the East Coast for the trip back to England.

In the summer of 1912 Chaplin and the Karno troupe were booked at the St. Helier Opera House in Jersey (The Channel Islands) as an attraction of the annual Battle of the Flowers festivities. After a matinee performance, Alf Reeves and Chaplin wandered along to the racetrack to watch the traditional procession of flower-covered floats. A newsreel photographer was filming the event and Charlie became curious about his camera. Then, realizing that it was pointed in his direction, he began an impromptu mime. A French child who happened to notice him tugged at his mother's sleeve and demanded, "Maman, je vieux voir encore ce comique." Alas, no one seems to know what became of that historic piece of film that captured Charlie's first performance in front of a movie camera! And no one now knows the identity of that prescient child who must be regarded as Chaplin's first movie fan.

Back in England, Charlie embarked on a fourteen-week tour of the London music halls. When that was over and Karno offered him the chance of a second American trip, he accepted without hesitation. This time (December 1912), he crossed the Atlantic as the established star of a repertoire of sketches of his own choosing.

His troupe was playing Philadelphia when his great moment of decision arrived. Alf Reeves handed him a telegram from New York that requested Chaplin to get in touch with Kessel and Bauman at 24 Longacre Building on Broadway. Charlie fancifully assumed that he had inherited a legacy from a long-lost relative. But on reaching New York he was disappointed to find that Kessel and Bauman were not attorneys but motion picture executives. (At this period he had a rather low opinion of the movies and knew nothing about the movie industry.)

Actually, Adam Kessel was president and Charles Bauman treasurer of the newly established Keystone Film Company. They were interested in Chaplin as a possible replacement for Ford Sterling, their leading comedian, who was quitting their company to produce his own comedies. Kessel and Bauman were prepared to offer Chaplin a weekly salary of $150 for which he would be expected to make a maximum of three one-reel pictures a week. This was twice the amount he was receiving from Karno, yet he hesitated. He had seen the kind of comedies that Keystone made and considered them "a crude mélange of rough and tumble." They seemed to him as inferior to the artistry of a polished Karno sketch as he had once thought the music hall was inferior to the lofty heights of the legitimate theater. On the other hand, he realized that movies had a considerable publicity value. "A year at that racket and I could return to vaudeville an international star. Besides, it would mean a new life and a pleasant environment."[53] He pondered the offer and then told the two executives that he could not consider it seriously unless they raised the salary to two hundred a week. He was quite unaware that Ford Sterling had asked Sennett for $750 before making up his mind to strike out on his own. He might otherwise have upped the ante even more—and would, to his surprise—have got most of what he asked for. But as it was, no sooner had he demanded $200 than he began to doubt his audacity and to ask himself whether the money (and what went with it) was what he really wanted. Meanwhile, Kessel and Bauman consulted with Sennett and came back with a counter-offer: a year's contract providing $150 for the first three months and $175 for the remaining nine.[59] For twenty-four-year-old Charles Spencer Chaplin this meant more money than he had ever been offered in his life. And so he scrawled his name at the foot of his first movie contract. But his misgivings remained. Had he done the right thing? What could the movies do for him that the theater had not?

As we know now, his career as a vaudeville star was at an end. His Sullivan and Considine tour concluded on November 28, 1913 when he played at the Empress Theater, Kansas City. On the eve of his departure from the theater, a local paper published this prophetic valediction:

> Charlie Chaplin, who numbers his friends by the thousand, is going to desert the stage to become a movie actor and play the chief comedy roles with the Keystone Company. As a film actor Charlie should surely make good, for during the five years he has been with the Karno Company, and on all

his visits to this city, he has not spoken a dozen lines, and has depended on facial expression and pantomime, the two secrets of success in the silent drama, to gain him the laughs. We shall all be anxiously awaiting the Keystone films in which he appears, and it goes without saying they will be just as funny as he has been in the various Karno offerings.[55]

Chaplin arrived in Los Angeles in December 1913 and took a streetcar to the Keystone film studios in Edendale. What followed is history.

NOTES

1. Raoul Sobel and David Francis, *Chaplin: Genesis of a Clown* (London: Quartet Books, 1977), p. 61.

2. *Ibid.*

3. Kalton C. Lahue, *Mack Sennett's Keystone* (South Brunswick: A. S. Barnes & Co., 1971), pp. 108–9.

4. John McCabe, *Charlie Chaplin* (New York: Doubleday, 1978), p. 90.

5. McCabe, p.x.

6. See G. J. Mellor, "The Making of Charlie Chaplin," "The Making of Charlie Chaplin," *Cinema Studies* II, no. 2 (June 1966), pp. 19–25.

7. *My Autobiography* (New York: Simon and Schuster, 1964), p. 45.

8. *My Autobiography*, p. 45.

9. On Dan Leno, see particularly Gyles Brandreth, *The Funniest Man on Earth* (London: Hamish Hamilton, 1977) and John Duncan, ed., *Dan Leno: hys booke* (London: Hugh Evelyn, 1968).

10. *My Autobiography*, p. 45.

11. Harold Scott, *The Early Doors* (London: n.d.), p. 175.

12. Robert Payne, *The Great God Pan* (New York: Hermitage House, 1953), p. 64.

13. George Le Roy, *Music Hall Stars of the Nineties* (London: British Technical and General Press, 1952), p. 14.

14. Scott, p. 176.

15. Short, p. 176.

16. *MA*, p. 50

17. Sobel and Francis, p. 66.

18. Denis Gifford in *The Movie Makers: Chaplin* (New York: Doubleday, 1974), p. 14, maintains that this gag suggests the formula for Chaplin's film comedy. "Its basis was incongruity: the simple switch. A cat behaving like its opposite, a dog. The behavior itself: fundamental, universal, lavatorial. . . . The form: visual. The gag needed no words of explanation. Above all, the spontaneity: the gag was unexpected. . . ."

19. See further Daniel Frohman, *Daniel Frohman Presents: An Autobiography* (New York: Kendall & Sharp, 1935), p. 292.

20. *MA*, p. 78.

21. Quoted in Gifford, p. 19.

22. *MA*, p. 81.

23. Quoted in Gifford, p. 19.

24. Several biographers have stated that Chaplin played one of the wolves in the first production of *Peter Pan*, which premiered at the Duke of York's, London, December 27, 1904. Roger Lancelyn Green, an authority on *Peter Pan*, remarks: "A persistent legend includes among the pack of wolves the then unknown boy actor, Charlie Chaplin, who was working for Frohman at that time, having just finished touring as Billy the page-boy in William Gillette's *Sherlock Holmes*, and being shortly to appear in another Sherlock Holmes play at the Duke of York's. In spite of the fact that his name is not mentioned in the programme, most of Chaplin's biographers accept his appearance as certain, and the issue has been complicated by the fact that he is said to have acted occasionally at this time under his second name of Spencer. The "S. Spencer" in the cast, however, was the negro who played the "Black Pirate" in every London revival until 1914. Charlie Chaplin might so easily have been in *Peter Pan*, even if he only replaced some other young actor for a few performances; but he himself has now stated that it is no more than a legend — which we must regretfully lay to rest" (*Fifty Years of Peter Pan*, London: Peter Davies, 1954, pp. 93–94). Unfortunately, Chaplin himself seems never to have made up his mind whether or not the story of his appearance in Barrie's play was really a legend. Three years after the publication of Green's statement, Chaplin told an interviewer for the London *Daily*

Herald (September 12, 1957): "I appeared in pantomime as a dog [sic] and in *Peter Pan* as a wolf. Might have got typed in zoological roles if I hadn't managed to get a legitimate part in a Sherlock Holmes play." It is possible, of course, that Chaplin played a wolf in one of the many *revivals* of *Peter Pan*, but is is almost a certainty that he did not appear in the premiere production.

25. Half a century later, Chaplin would recall Postance in the character of Postant (Nigel Bruce), the theatre impresario of *Limelight*.

26. See *CCOS*, ch. I, n. 6.

27. *MA*, p. 94.

28. Quoted in Gifford, p. 20.

29. See further *CCOS*, XXI and XXII.

30. *The New York Times*, September 25, 1921, VI, p. 3.

31. *The Era*, May 19, 1906, p. 6.

32. Advertisements in the various theater and music hall journals refer to Bodie as the human resistance coil, the world's greatest electrician, and the British Edison who allows three million volts to pass through his body. (See for example *The Era*, December 24, 1904, p. 35.) Aside from Chaplin's depiction of the amazing doctor, there was a notable literary characterization of him in J. M. Barrie's play, *A Kiss for Cinderella* (1916).

33. See *CCOS*, XXI and XXII.

34. Edwin Adeler and Con West, *Remember Fred Karno?* (London: John Long, 1939), p. 127.

35. The character was recreated years later by George Davis in Chaplin's film, *The Circus* (1928).

36. Chaplin, *My Trip Abroad* (New York & London: Harper & Brothers 1922), p. 161.

38. Recreated by Chaplin in his Mutual film, *The Rink* (1916).

39. *Yorkshire Evening Post*, July 23, 1910 (unpaginated press clipping in British Film Institute microfiche on Chaplin).

40. *Bradford Daily Argus*, August 27, 1910, p. 4.

41. See James P. O'Donnell, "Charlie Chaplin's Stormy Exile," *Saturday Evening Post*, March 8, 1958, p. 21.

42. See *CCOS*, I, n. 12.

43. See Chaplin, *My Life in Pictures* (New York: Grosset & Dunlap, 1975), pp. 41, 54–55.

44. Gifford, p. 26.

45. Contrast the Tramp's "arrival at the Land of Liberty" in Chaplin's Mutual film *The Immigrant* (1917).

46. *MA*, p. 119.

47. *Photoplay*, February 1915 (unpaginated press clipping in New York Public Library file on Chaplin).

48. Quoted in Gifford, p. 27.

49. See *CCOS*, XXIII, n. 1.

50. *Los Angeles Examiner*, May 21, 1912 (unpaginated press clipping in New York Public Library file on Chaplin).

51. *Vancouver News*, April 12, 1919 (N.Y. Public Library file).

52. Mack Sennett and Cameron Shipp, *King of Comedy* (New York: Pinnacle Books, 1975), p. 148.

53. *MA*, p. 138.

54. Kalton Lahue has noted: "Many claimed to have discovered Chaplin's screen potential. It is impossible now to determine with any certainty who really recommended him to whom, and why. . . . Terry Ramsaye asserts Adam Kessel discovered Chaplin . . . Sennett took credit for discovering Chaplin late in 1912, and telephoning Kessel and Charles Bauman a few days later with a request that they locate the unknown Englishman he had seen; Fred Balshofer and Chaplin both state that Charles Kessel [Adam's brother] caught Charlie's act and was the man responsible for talking Adam Kessel and Charles Bauman into hiring the little Englishman" (Lahue, *Mack Sennett's Keystone*, South Brunswick: A. S. Barnes, 1971, p. 109). See also "How Pictures Found Charlie," *Photoplay*, April 1919 (unpaginated press clipping in New York Public Library file).

55. Undated clipping in British Film Institute microfiche on Chaplin.

Charlie Chaplin's Own Story

Being the faithful recital of a romantic career, beginning
with early recollections of boyhood in London
and closing with the signing of his latest
motion-picture contract

CONTENTS

CONTENTS

CONTENTS

In which I relate my experiences up to the age of five; and describe the occasion of my first public appearance on any stage.

Life itself is a comedy — a slap-stick comedy at that. It is always hitting you over the head with the unexpected. You reach to get the thing you want — slap! bang! It's gone! You strike at your enemy and hit a friend. You walk confidently, and fall. Whether it is tragedy or comedy depends on how you look at it.[1] There is not a hair's breadth between them.

When I was eleven years old, homeless and starving in London, I had big dreams. I was a precocious youngster, full of imagination and fancies and pride. My dream was to become a great musician,[2] or an actor like Booth.[3] Here I am to-day, becoming a millionaire[4] because I wear funny shoes. Slap-stick comedy, what?

Still, there is not much laughter in the world, and a lot of that is cynical. As long as I can keep people laughing good chuckling laughs I shall be satisfied. I can't keep it up long, of course. The public is like a child; it gets tired of its toys and throws them away.[5] When that happens I shall do something else, and still be satisfied. I always knew that some day I would have my share of the spot-light, and I am having it, so after all I have realized my ambitions.

My mother is proud of it. That is another of life's slap-stick comedies—that my mother, one of the proudest, most gentle women in England, should hope for twenty years that some day I would be a great tragic actor, and now should lie in an English hospital,[6] glad that I am greeted with howls of laughter whenever I appear in comedy make-up on the moving-picture screen.

When I was two or three years old my mother began to be proud of my acting. After she and my father came back from their work in the London music-halls they used to have little parties of friends for supper, and father would come and pull me out of bed to stand on the table and recite for them.

My father was a great, dark, handsome man.[7] He would put me upon his shoulder to bring me out, and I did not like it, because his rough prickly cheek hurt me. Then he would set me upon the table in my nightgown, with the bright light hurting my eyes, and every one would laugh and tell me to sing for the drops of wine in their glasses. I always did, and the party applauded and laughed and called for more. I could mimic every one I had ever seen and sing all the songs I had heard.

They would keep me doing it for hours, until I got so sleepy I could not stand up and fell over among the dishes. Then mother picked me up and and carried me to bed again. I remember just how her hair fell down over the pillow as she tucked me in. It was brown hair, very soft and perfumed, and her face was so full of fun it seemed to sparkle. That was in the early days, of course.

I do not know my mother's real name. She came of a good respected family in London, and when she was sixteen she ran away and married my father, a music-hall actor.[8] She never heard from her own people again. She drifted over England and the Continent with my father, and went on the music-hall stage herself. They never made much money, and my father spent it all.[9] Most of the time we lived very poorly,[10] in actors' lodgings, and my mother worried about food for us. Then there would be a streak of luck, and we all had new clothes and lived lavishly for a few days.

My brother Sydney[11] was four years old when I was born in a little town in France,[12] between music-hall engagements. As soon as my mother could travel we went back to London, and she went to work again. Her stage name was Lily Harley,[13] and she was very popular in English music-halls, where she sang character songs.[14] She had a beautiful sweet voice, but she hated the stage and the life. Sometimes at night she came into my bed and cried herself to sleep with her arms around me, and I was so miserable that I wanted to scream, but I did not dare, for fear of waking my father.

He was Charles Chaplin, the singer of descriptive ballads.[15] His voice was a fine baritone, and he was a great music-hall success and is still remembered in England. My mother and he were always laughing and singing together, and my mother was very fond of him, but a little afraid, too. When he was angry she grew white and her hands shook. She had thin delicate hands, which reminded me of the claws of some little bird when she dressed me.

In spite of the hit-and-miss life we led, always moving from town to town, and my mother's hard work on the stage and our lack of money, she took pride in keeping my brother and me beautifully dressed. At night, after her music-hall work was done and the party had gone, I woke and saw her pressing out our little white Eton collars and brushing our suits, while every one was asleep.

One day, when I was about five years old, Sydney and I were playing on the floor when my mother came in, staggering. I thought she was drunk. I had seen so many persons drunk it was commonplace to me, but seeing my mother that way was horrible. I opened my mouth and screamed in terror. I screamed and screamed; it seemed as if I could not stop.

Sydney ran out of the room. My mother did not look at me; she stumbled across the room and tried to take off her hat. All her hair came tumbling down over her face, and she fell on the bed.

After a while I crawled over and touched her hand, which

hung down. It was cold, and it frightened me so I could not make a sound. I backed under the bed, little by little, until I reached the wall, and sat there, still, staring at my mother's hand.

After a long time the door opened and I saw my father's boots walk in. I heard him swearing. The boots came over and stood by the bed. I smelled whisky, and after a while I heard my mother's voice, very weak.

"Don't be a hysterical fool. You've got to work tonight. We need the money," my father said.

"I can't. I'm not up to it. I'm sick," I heard my mother say, sobbing.

My father's boots stamped up and down the room.

"Well, I'll take Charlie, then," he said. "Where's the brat?"

I backed closer to the wall, and kept still. With no reason, I was terrified. Then the door opened again, my father's boots tramped out and down the stairs, and I heard my mother calling me. I came slowly out from under the bed.

My mother said she wanted me to go on the stage in her place that night and sing my very best. I said I would. Then she had me bring her a little new coat she had made for me, and a fresh collar. She still lay on the bed, and my chin barely came above the edge of it, so it took her a long time to dress me and to get my hair combed to suit her. She was still busy with it when my father came back.

Then she kissed me in a hurry and told me to do my best. My father took my hand and we started to the music-hall. We were at Aldershot,[16] a garrison town, and soldiers were everywhere. I kept tipping my head back to see their uniforms as they passed us, and my father was jerking me along at such a rate my neck nearly snapped in two.

We were late when we reached the music-hall. I had never seen one before; my mother had always put us to bed before

4

she went to work. My father took me down a little alley, through a bare dim place, to one end of the stage. I saw a big crowd on the other side of it—just hundreds of heads massed together. There were music and noise, and the stage was a glare of light.

A girl in tights and shiny spangles came and put grease paint on my cheeks, and when I wanted to rub it off they would not let me. Then it was time for my mother's act, and my father faced me toward the stage and gave me a little push.

"Go out and sing *Jack Jones*," he said.[17]

In which I make my first public appearance on the stage and my first success; and meet the red-faced man.

I walked uncertainly out of the lights dazzled me seemed a great empty alone. I did not know 2 on the stage. The glare so I stumbled. The stage place, and I felt little and just what to do, but my father had told me to go out and sing *Jack Jones*, and I did not dare go back until I had done it.

There was a great uproar beyond the footlights, and it confused me more, until I saw that the people were laughing and applauding. Then I remembered my singing on the table, with people all around and noise and light, and I saw that this was the same thing. I opened my mouth and sang *Jack Jones* with all my might.

It was an old coster song my father had taught me. I sang one verse and started on the second, hurrying to get through. I was not afraid of the crowd, but the stage got bigger and I got littler every minute, and I wanted to be with my mother.

There was a great noise which interrupted my song, and something hit me on the cheek. I stopped singing with my mouth open on a note, and something else hit the floor by my feet, and then a shower of things fell on the stage and one struck my arm. The audience was throwing them at me.

I backed away a little terrified, but I went on singing as well as I could, with my face quivering and a big lump in my throat. I knew I had to finish the song because my father had told me to. Great tears came up in my eyes, and I ducked my head and rubbed at them with my knuckles, and then I saw the floor of the stage. It was almost covered with pennies and shillings. Money! It was money they were throwing at me!

"Oh! Wait, wait!" I shouted, and went down on my hands and knees to gather it up. "It's money! Wait just a minute!"

I got both hands full of it, and still there was more. I crawled around, picking it up and putting it in my pockets and shouted at the audience, "Wait till I get it all and I'll sing a lot!"

It was a great hit. People laughed and shouted and climbed on their seats to throw more money. It kept falling around me, rolling across the stage, while I ran after it, shouting with joy. I filled all my pockets and put some in my hat. Then I stood up and sang *Jack Jones* twice, and would have sung it again, but my father came out on the stage and led me off.

I had almost three pounds in six-penny pieces, shillings, and even a few half-crowns. I sat on a box and played with it while my father did his act. I could not count it, but I knew it was money, and I felt rich. Then we went home, where my father set me upon the bed beside my mother, and I poured the money over her, laughing. She laughed, too, and my father took the money and bought us all a great feast, and let me drink some of the ale. I remember how I crowed over Sydney that night.[1]

My mother was able to go back to work next day, and Sydney and I were left in the rooms again. There was a quarrel before she went; my father swore, and mother cried and stamped her foot. She said, "No! No! No! He's too little yet." And I knew they were talking about me, and crawled away into a corner, where I kept very still.

After that I think we grew poorer and poorer. There were no more parties at night. My mother would come in alone, and when she waked me, tucking me in, I felt so sad it seemed as if my heart would break, because her face did not sparkle any more. Sydney and I played about in the daytime, and kept out of father's way. When he came in his face was red, and his breath was hot and strong with whisky. He used to throw himself on the bed without a word to mother and fall asleep with his mouth open. Then Sydney and I went quietly out and played on the stairs. Sydney was a wide-awake lively young person, always running about and shouting "Ship ahoy!" He wanted to be a sailor.[2] I could not play with him long because it tired me. I liked to get into a corner by myself and think and dream of things I had seen and what I would do some day— vague dreams of making music and wearing velvet suits and bowing to immense audiences and having cream tarts for every meal and six white ponies to drive.

The worry and the unhappiness which seemed to grow like a cloud around us in those years made me sit sometimes and cry quietly to myself, not knowing why, but feeling miserable and sad. Then my great dreams faded and I felt little and lonely, and not even my mother could comfort me.

So I came to be about ten years old, and all my memories of the years between my first appearance on the stage and the day I met the red-faced man are vague recollections of these dreams and hurried trips from place to place, and the unhappiness, and my mother's face growing sadder. Then I remember clearly the night I went with her to the music-hall in London and ran away with the clog dancers.[3]

My mother took me with her because when it was time for her to go to work she could not find Sydney. He was almost fourteen and played a great deal in the streets, and used to go away for the whole day sometimes, which worried my mother. But she had to work and could not be with us or keep us together. It is my impression that my father was making very little money then, and spending all he got in bars, as he was a very popular man and had many friends who wanted him to drink with them. I know that we were living in very poor lodgings, and my mother cried sometimes when the landlady asked her for the rent.

I remember on this day standing beside my mother and watching a troupe of clog dancers who were working on the stage. Mother was wearing her stage dress, waiting to go on for her act, and she kept asking me where I had seen Sydney last, but I could hardly listen. I knew how to clog dance, for Sydney and I had done it with the boys in the streets, and I was impatient because my mother had her hand on my shoulder, and I wanted to do the steps with the others. I squirmed away from her and began dancing by myself. I did all the difficult steps very proudly, and when the music stopped I saw that my mother looked proud, too. I looked around to see if any one else was admiring me, and saw the red-faced man.

He was standing behind my mother, a fat man, with a double chin, and a wart on one of his lower eyelids. It fascinated me so I could not take my eyes from it. When my mother went on for her act I still stood staring at it.

"I say, you're lively on your feet, young feller," he said to me. "Could you do that every day, say?"

"Oh, yes, I like to do it," I said.

"Would you like to come along, now, with a nice troupe of fine little boys and do it for a fortnight or so?" he asked.

"What's the screw?" I said, looking shrewd, as I had seen my father do. He laughed.

"Three six a week," he said, "all for your own pocket money. And I'll buy you a velvet suit, and you can eat hearty— meat pies and pudding every meal."

"And cream tarts?" I stipulated.

"Up to your eyes in cream tarts if you like," he said. "Come now, will you do it?"

"Yes," I answered promptly.

"All right, come along," he said, and led me out of the music-hall.

9

In which I join the clog dancers; fail to get the cream tarts; and incur the wrath of Mr. Hawkins.

Waiting just inside the door to the alley were the five boys who had been clog dancing.[1] They were huddled together, not playing or talking, and when the red-faced man led me up to them they looked at me curiously, without a word. Each one had his stage dress in a brown paper bundle under his arm, and in the gas light they looked ragged and tired.

"This 'ere's the new little boy what's a-going to come with us," said the red-faced man, holding my hand so tight it hurt, and I squirmed.

The other boys did not say a word. They looked at me, and all those staring eyes made me uncomfortable.

"Speak up, there!" roared the man suddenly, and they all jumped. "Say 'Yes, sir, yes, Mr. 'Awkins,'[2] when I speak to you!"

"Yes, sir, yes, Mr. 'Awkins!" they all said.

"Now step up, young fellers; we're going to our nice 'ome and 'ave cream tarts for our supper," Mr. Hawkins said. He nodded to the stage doorkeeper, a silent whiskered man who sat smoking a pipe, and we all filed out through the dark little alley into the street.

It was a cold foggy night.[3] The street lamps were weird ghostly-looking blurs in the mist, and our steps sounded hollow and muffled. I had never been out so late before, and the strange look of things in the fog and the emptiness of the streets, with only a cab rattling by now and then, made me shiver.

The boys walked ahead, and Mr. Hawkins and I followed close behind. We walked for a long time, till my legs began to

10

ache and my fingers stopped hurting and grew numb in Mr. Hawkins' hard grip. My mind was all a-muddle and confused, so that the only thing I thought of clearly was my mother, and how pleased she would be when I came home again rich, with three and sixpence and a velvet suit.

We came at last to a doorway with a lamp burning dimly over it, and Mr. Hawkins herded the boys into it. A very fat dirty woman opened the door and said something shrill to us. Then we climbed many flights of dark stairs, and Mr. Hawkins let go my hand to open a door.

A damp musty smell came out as we stumbled in. It was a poor dirty room, furnished with two beds and a long table with chairs about it.

"Well, 'ere we are 'ome!" said Mr. Hawkins cheerfully. "Now for a nice 'ot supper, what?" The boys did not say a word. They sat down and watched him, looking now and then at the door. I rubbed my aching fingers and looked at him, too. The wart was still there on his lower eyelid, and I could not take my eyes from it.

After a while the fat woman came in with our supper—chops and ale for Mr. Hawkins; plates of porridge and thick slices of bread for us. The boys all fell to eating hungrily, but I pushed my plate back and looked at Mr. Hawkins, who was eating his chops and drinking his ale with great enjoyment.

"Where are the cream tarts?" I asked him.

"Cream tarts! Who ever 'eard of cream tarts for supper?" he shouted. "Cream tarts!" He chuckled and repeated it over and over, till I felt ashamed and confused. Then he thrust his great red face almost against mine and roared in a terrible voice, "That's enough, young feller! I'll cream tart you! I'll jolly well cream tart you!" I shrank into my chair, frightened.

"You don't want cream tarts," he said. "You want a caning. You want a good hard caning, don't you?"

"No, sir," I said. "Oh, no, sir, please."

11

"Oh, you don't, don't you? Yes, you do. You want a caning, that's what you want. Where's my cane?" he roared in a frightful voice. I crouched in my chair in such terrible fear I could not even cry out until his great hand gripped my shoulder. Then I shrieked in agony.

He only shook me and flung me back in the chair, but from that moment I lived in terror of him—a terror that colored everything during the day and at night made my dreams horrible. The other boys were afraid of him, too. When he was with us we sat silent and wary, looking at him. He used to swing his cane as he walked up and down the room in the evenings, and we watched it in fearful fascination, though I do not remember that he ever caned one of us. It was the constant fear of his doing it that was so terrible. Sometimes when he had locked us in the room and gone away in the morning the boldest boys used to make fantastic threats of the things they would do to him when he returned, but they said them under their breath, with an eye on the door, and the rest of us quaked as we listened.

In the evenings we were marched out before him to music-halls. These music-halls were different from the ones my mother sang in. They were large rooms, with rough wooden benches and tables arranged around a square in the center, where we danced. The air was thick with tobacco smoke and heavy with the smell of ale and stout, and the ugly bearded faces of hundreds of men staring at us confused me sometimes so that I could hardly dance. I was so little, so weary from hunger and the constant fear of Mr. Hawkins, that my feet felt too heavy to lift in the hard steps, and my head swam in the glare of the lights. I wanted so much to crawl away to a quiet dark place where I could rest and feel my mother's hand tucking in the covers, that sometimes I sobbed as I danced, but I never stopped nor missed a step; I did not dare.

For all the pain and fear in my childish heart I did the steps very well, so that often the crowd cheered "the young 'un" and called for more. Then, while they shouted and banged their mugs of ale on the tables, I would wearily dance again and again, until all my body ached. Sometimes they threw money to me, and then, after they let me go at last, Mr. Hawkins would go through my pockets for it and rap my head with his knuckles, under the suspicion that I had concealed some.

All my memory of those weeks is colored by my terror of him. It never left me. When he was in the room I got as far as possible from him and sat quite still, staring at his face and the wart on his eyelid and his great cane. When he was gone I sat and brooded about him and shivered. At the table, hungry as I was, I could not swallow my porridge under the gaze of his awful eye.

At last one night when we reached the music-hall where we were to dance we found it in great uproar. The audience was standing on benches and tables and shouting, "Slug 'im! Slug 'im! Slug 'im!" in horrible waves of sound. In the center, where we were to dance, two men were fighting.

Mr. Hawkins pushed us before him through the crowd to a place close to them. I saw their strong naked bodies glistening under the gas flare and heard the terrible smashing blows. There was a sweetish sickening smell in the air which made me feel ill, and the roar of the crowd terrified me. Then one of the men reeled, staggered backward and fell. He was close to me and I saw his face, a shapeless mass of flesh, with no eyes, covered with blood, with blood running from the open mouth. The horror of it struck my childish mind so, after all those weeks of terror, that I fainted.

I was revived in time to dance, and the crowd, excited by the fight, threw us a great deal of money. When he searched my pockets at the door, Mr. Hawkins stooped low, put his great face almost against mine and swore, but he did not rap me with his knuckles. I was in a kind of stupor, quivering all over, and could not walk, so he put me up on his shoulder, as my father used to do, and started home.

A long time afterward I knew I was standing between his knees, while he tipped my head back and looked closely at me.

"Hingratitude, that's wot it is," he said fiercely. "Speak up, young 'un. Don't you 'ave a-plenty to eat of good 'olesome porridge? Don't you 'ave a good kind master wot never canes yer?"

"Oh, yes, sir," I said, in a panic of fear.

"Then don't you go a-being ungrateful, and a-dying on my 'ands, like young Jim done," he roared at me furiously. "You 'ear? Stubbornness, that's wot it is. I won't 'ave it!"

In which I feel very small and desolate; encounter once more the terrible wrath of Mr. Hawkins; and flee from it into the unknown perils of a great and fearful world.

"It's stubbornness, that's Mr. Hawkins said fierce- cane.

4

wot it is! I won't 'ave it!" ly, and reached for his

I struggled in the grip of his great knees, and cried in terror that I did not mean it, I was sorry, I would be good. I begged him not to beat me. Even when he let me go I could not stop screaming.

It must have been some time next day that I woke in a hot tumbled bed. I thought my mother had been there, with her hair falling over the pillow and her face all sparkling with fun. I put up my arms with a cry, and she was gone. A strange ugly girl, with a broom in her hand, was leaning over me.

"Coom, coom,"[1] she said crossly, shaking my shoulder. "Wark's to be done. No time to be lyin' a-bed."

I struggled to get away from her heavy hand, and sobbed that I wanted my mother, I wanted to go home. I was so little and so miserable and weary that the grief of missing my mother seemed almost to break my heart.

"She's gone," the girl said, still pulling at me. "She willna be vexed wi' a girt[2] boy, weeping like a baaby."

"No! No!" I screamed at her. "My mother hasn't gone away. My mother hasn't left me."

"Yus, she has," the girl told me. "She's gone."

I let her lift me from the bed then, and sat limp on the floor where she put me, leaning my aching head against the bedpost. All my childish courage and hope was gone, and I was left very little and alone in a terrible black world where my mother did not care for me any more. I sat there desolate, with

15

great tears running down my cheeks, and did not wish to stir or move or ever see any one again.

Long hours later, after it had been dark a long time, Mr. Hawkins came in with the boys, and I had no strength even to fear him. When he roared at me I still sat there and only trembled and turned my head away. I remember his walking up and down and looking at me a long time, and I remember his holding a mug of ale to my lips and making me swallow some, but everything was confused and vague, and I did not care for anything, only wanting to be left alone.

It may have been the next day, or several days later, that we were all walking over rough cobbled streets, very early in the morning, in a cold thick fog. I walked unsteadily, because my legs felt limp, and Mr. Hawkins held my hand tight, so that my arm ached. We were all going to a fair in the country. I was interested in that, because my mother had once taken Sydney and me to a meadow, where we all played in the grass and found cowslips and ate cakes from a basket under a tree.

After we had walked a long time Mr. Hawkins took us into an eating-house, where we had a breakfast of sausages and I drank a big mug of hot coffee. When we came out the sun was shining and we walked down a wide white road, past many great houses with grass and trees about them. I had never imagined such places, and with the delight of seeing them, and the sunlight and the good breakfast, I felt better, and thought I could walk by myself if Mr. Hawkins would let go my hand, though I dared not speak of it.

As we walked on, the road grew busy with carriages coming and going and farmers' wagons coming in to market, and after a time a coster's cart overtook us, and Mr. Hawkins bargained with the driver to carry us.

Then I began to be almost happy again, as I sat in the back of the cart with my legs dangling and saw the road unrolling backward between the wheels. It was a warm morning; the road was thick with white dust, and the smell of it and of the green fields, to which we came presently, and all the country sights and sounds, were pleasant. We drove for miles between the hedgerows, and I grew quite excited looking for the five-barred gates in them, through which we caught glimpses of the farms on either side. So at last we came to Barnet,[3] where the fair was to be.

The village looked bright and clean, with red brick buildings standing close to the narrow street, and shining white cobblestones. We all climbed down before the inn, and I looked eagerly for meadows, but there were none. Mr. Hawkins hurried us to the field where the fair had already begun. It was crowded with tents and people, and there was a great noise of music and shouting and cries of hokey-pokey men and venders.

"Step lively now, young 'uns," ordered Mr. Hawkins in an awful voice. "'Ustle into them velveteen smalls, and get your jackets on in a 'urry, or I'll show you wot's wot!"

We dressed in mad haste in a little tent, and he had us into a larger one and hard at work dancing in no time. We heard his voice outside, shouting loud over the uproar of the crowd, "'Ere! 'Ere! This way for the Lunnon clog dancers! Only a penny! See the grite Lunnon clog dancers!" A few people came in, then more, and more, till the tent was full of them, coming and going.

It was hard work dancing; my feet felt heavy to lift and my stomach ached with hunger, but I did not dare stop a minute. I danced on and on, in that hot and stuffy place, with a fearful eye on the tent-flap, where now and again Mr. Hawkins' red face appeared and glared at us, and we saw his hand with the cane gripped in it.

Over and over we did the steps, while the tent grew hotter, and laughing people came and stared and went away, until my

17

breath came in gasps and my head swam and grew large, and larger, and then very tiny again, in a most confusing manner. Then everything went black and I must have fallen, for Mr. Hawkins was shaking me where I lay on the ground, and saying to some one, "'E's all right. 'E's only wilful; 'e wants a good caning, 'e does."

After that I was dancing again, but I did not see the crowd any more. I only danced, and longed for the time when I might stop.

It came after a long, long while. The tent was cooler and empty when Mr. Hawkins came in and took me by the shoulder, and my head cleared so that I saw I need dance no more. My weary muscles gave way and I sat on the floor, looking at him fearfully while he wiped his face with his handkerchief.

"You, with yer woite faces!" he roared hoarsely. "'Ow many times 'ave I told yer to look cheery while you dance? I've a mind to cane the lot of yer!" We trembled. "But I won't," he said, after a dreadful pause. "We're all a-goin' hover to the inn and 'ave bread and cheese."

He took my hand again and we dragged wearily over to the inn, a bright clean place, with sawdust on the floor. It was crowded with men, and they greeted us with loud voices as we came in.

"'Ere's the Lunnon clog dancers, come to dance for bread and cheese," Mr. Hawkins said cheerfully. He looked at the barmaid, who nodded, and a place was cleared for us to begin our weary dancing again.

My tired little legs would hardly hold me up, and I stumbled in the steps. Under the terrible eye of Mr. Hawkins I did my best, panting with fear, but I could not dance. I stopped at last, and leaned against the bar. Mr. Hawkins reached for me, but as I shrank back with a cry I felt warm arms around me. It was the barmaid who held me, and after one look at her red cheeks, so close, I began to cry on her shoulder.

"Pore little dear, 'e's tired," she said, holding me tight from Mr. Hawkins. "'E shall 'ave his bread and cheese without 'is dancing." "'E's a wilful, perverse hungrateful creetur!" Mr. Hawkins said, but she did not seem to mind. She took me behind the bar and gave me a scorching drink of something and a great piece of bread which I was too weary to eat. Afterward Mr. Hawkins took me back to the fair, jerking me furiously along by the arm. He took me to the little tent where we had dressed and put me inside.

"I'll tike the 'ide off you when I come back," he said hoarsely, bending to bring his red face close to mine. "I'll give you a caning wot *is* a caning, I will. I've been too gentle with you, I 'ave. You stay 'ere, and wait."

With these dreadful words and a horrible oath he went away, and I could hear him shouting before the other tent above the sounds of the evening's merrymaking. "'Ere! 'Ere! This way to the Lunnon clog dancers! Only a penny!"

I was left in such a state of misery and wretchedness, shaking with such fear, that not even my great weariness would let me sleep. I sat there in the dark for a long time, trembling, and then, driven by terror of Mr. Hawkins' return, I crawled beneath the edge of the tent and set out blindly to get beyond the reach of his voice.

When I came to the edge of the crowd I ran as fast as I could.

In which I have an adventure
with a cow; become a lawless filcher of
brandysnaps; [1] and confound an honest farmer.

I ran for a long time in the darkness, blindly, not caring where I went, only that I escaped from Mr. Hawkins. The pounding of my heart shook me as I plunged across fields and scrambled under gates in my way, until at last I came to a corner of two hedges, and had no strength to go farther. I curled myself into as small a space as possible, close to the hedges, and lay there. It seemed to me that I was hidden and safe, and I was quite content as I went to sleep.

Early in the morning I was awakened by a curious swishing noise, and saw close to my face the great staring eyes of a strange animal. It was a cow, but I had never seen one, and I thought it was one of the giants my mother had told about. I saw its tongue, lapping up about its nose, and as I stared it licked my face. The moist sandpapery feeling of it startled me and I howled.

At the sound it backed away with a snort, and so we remained, staring at each other for a long time. It was a bright morning, with birds singing in the hedgerows, and if it had not been for my hunger and an uneasiness lest the cow meant to lick me again I would have been quite happy, so far from Mr. Hawkins.

Then between me and the cow came a woman with a big bucket on her arm, carrying a three-legged stool. Quite fearlessly she slapped the great animal, and it turned meekly and stood, while she sat on the stool and began to milk. It was the strangest thing I had ever seen, and I went over to her side and stood watching the thin white stream pattering on the bottom of the bucket. She gave a great start and cried out in surprise when she saw me.

"Lawk a mussy!"[2] she said, and sat with her mouth open. I must have been a strange sight in that farmyard, a thin little child—for I was only ten and very small for that age—in velveteen smalls and a round jacket with tinsel braid on it.

"Where did you coom from?" she asked.

"I come from London. I am an actor," I said importantly. "What are you doing?" and pointed to the bucket.

She laughed at that and seeing, I suppose, that I looked hungry, she held the bucket to my lips, and I tasted the fresh warm milk. I drank every drop, in great delight. I had never tasted anything so delicious before.

"Are you hungry?" she asked me, and I told her solemnly, believing it, that I had had nothing to eat for a week. Her consternation at that was so great she dropped the bucket, but hastily picking it up, she sat down and milked again until she had another huge draught for me. Then she finished the milking in a hurry and took me into the farmhouse kitchen, a bright place, with shining pans on the wall and a pleasant smell of cooking.

The tale I told the farmer's wife I do not remember, but she took me up in her arms, saying, "Poor little lad! Poor little lad!" over and over, while she felt my thin arms, and I squirmed, for I did not like to be pitied, and besides, I saw the breakfast on the table and wished she would let me have some. When she set me down before it at last I could hardly wait to begin, while, to my surprise, she tied a napkin around my neck.

It was a mighty breakfast—porridge and eggs, with a rasher of bacon and marmalade, and the maid who had milked the cow was cutting great slices of crusty bread and butter. But before I had taken up a spoon the farmer came in. He was a big bluff man, and at sight of me he began to ask questions in a loud voice.

"Well, my lad, where did you come from?" he said.

"From the fair, sir," I answered, eager to be at the food, and not thinking what I said.

"Oh, 'e's the little lad wi' the clog dancers I told you of, Mary," he said. "Gi' him breakfuss, if you like, and I'll be takin' him back to his master as I go to the village."

At the terrible thought of Mr. Hawkins, whom I had almost forgotten, panic took me. I sat there trembling for a second, and then, before a hand could be reached to stay me, I leaped from my chair and fled from the kitchen, through the farmyard and out the gate, the napkin fluttering at my neck. A long way down the lane I stopped, panting, and looked to see if any one was following me. No one was.

I wandered on for some time, growing hungrier with every step and regretting passionately the loss of the great breakfast before I saw the girl with the brandysnaps. She was a fat round-cheeked little girl, with her hair in braids, and she was swinging on a gate, humming to herself and nibbling a cookie. Others were piled on the gatepost beside her. I stopped and looked eagerly at them and at her. Badly as I wanted some I would not ask for them, and she looked at me round-eyed and said nothing.

So we eyed each other, until finally she made a face and stuck out her tongue at me. Then she opened her mouth wide and popped in a brandysnap. It was too much. With a yell I sprang at her and seized the cookies. She tumbled from the gate, and as she fell she howled appallingly. At the sound a great shaggy dog came bounding, and I fled in panic, clutching the brandysnaps.

The dog pursued me as I ran, in great leaps, my ears filled

with the fearful sound of his barks. I sped around a turn in the lane and saw before me a farmer's wagon going slowly along. The dog was hard on my heels. I caught a glimpse of his great red mouth and tongue. With a last panting effort I clambered upon the tail of the wagon and dived beneath the burlap which covered the load.

There, lying in the dimness among green vegetables, I consumed the brandysnaps to the last crumb, listening to the farmer's bewildered expostulation with the honest dog, which continued barking at the wagon until the farmer dismounted and pursued him down the road with his whip. Then, as the wagon went onward again, I ate a number of radishes and a raw potato, and experimentally bit the squash and marrows until, with a contented stomach, I curled up among the lettuce and fell asleep.

I was awakened by the stopping of the wagon and heard the farmer, busied with the horse, exchanging jovial greetings with other gruff voices. Undecided what to do, I lay still until I heard him speaking loudly almost over my head.

"I lay these are the finest vegetables ever come to market," he said proudly, and tore the burlap covering from me. I sat up.

There never was a more surprised farmer. He stood openmouthed. While the men around him laughed, I scrambled from among the vegetables over the wagon's edge and dived into the uproar of Covent Garden market.[3] Horses, donkeys, wagons, men, women and children crowded the place; on every side were piles of vegetables and bright fruit, and there was a clamor of laughter, shouts and the cries of hucksters.

I ran about, happy in all the confusion, and glad to feel London about me again. After a while I met a man who gave me a penny for helping him unload his vegetables, and I wandered out of the market and down the dirty cobbled streets outside. There was a barrel organ which I followed for a time, and then I met a hokey-pokey man[4] and spent my penny for his sweets. I felt as rich as a lord as I sat on the curb in the sunshine eating them.

**In which I come home again;
accustom myself to going to bed hungry;
and have an unexpected encounter with my father.**

As I sat there in the hokey-pokey for which I ny all my old dreams agined myself rich and **6** sunshine eating the had spent my only pen-came back to me. I imfamous, bowing before cheering audiences, wearing a tall silk hat and a cane, and buying my mother a silk dress.

It was a rough dirty street, swarming with ragged children and full of heavy vans driven by swearing drivers, but reality did not interfere with my dreams. It never has.

When I had licked the last sweetness of the cream from my fingers I rose and walked with a haughty swagger, raising my eyebrows disdainfully. It was difficult to look down on a person whose waistband was on a level with my eyes, but I managed it. Then I amused myself walking behind people and imitating them, until I heard a barrel organ and followed it, dancing with the other children.

I was adventurous and gay that morning, with no cares in the world. What did it matter that I had no food nor shelter nor friends in all London? I did not think of that.

It was late that afternoon, and I had wandered a long way, when my increasing hunger began to damp my spirits. My feet dragged before the windows of pastry shops, and the fruit on the street stands tempted me. When it grew dark and the gas lamps were lighted I felt very little and lonely again and longed to cry. The streets were crowded with people hurrying home — women with market baskets, and rough men, but no one noticed me. I was only a ragged hungry child, and there are thousands of them in London.

25

At last I stood forlorn before a baker's window looking at the cakes and buns inside and wanting them with all my heart. I stood there a long time, jostled by people going by, till a woman stopped beside me to look in also. Something about her skirt and shoes gave me a wild hope, and I looked up. It was my mother. My mother!

I clasped her about the knees and screamed. Then I felt her arms tight about me and she was kneeling beside me while we sobbed together. My mother, my dear mother, at last. She had not gone away; she had not forgotten me; she wanted me as much as ever. I clutched her, shaking and sobbing, as if I could never let go, until, little as she was, she picked me up and carried me home.

She was not living in actors' lodging any more; she had a poor little room in Palermo Terrace, Kensington — a room little better than the dreadful one where Mr. Hawkins had kept me — but it was like Heaven to me to be there, with my mother. I clung to her a long time, hysterical when she tried to take my arms from her neck, and we laughed and cried together while she petted and comforted me.

Neither my father nor Sydney was there, nor was there any sign that they were expected. When I was quieter, sitting on her lap eating a bun and tea, my mother said that they were gone. On the day I ran away with Mr. Hawkins, Sydney had gone to sea. My mother had a note from him, telling her about his grand place as steward's assistant on a boat going to Africa, and promising to bring her back beautiful presents and money. She had not heard from him again.

She undressed me with her tiny hands that reminded me of birds' claws and tucked me in bed, just as I had dreamed so often, with her soft hair falling over the pillow, and I went to sleep, my heart almost bursting with happiness at being home again.

When I woke in the morning, so early that it was not yet light, I saw her sitting beside a lamp, sewing. All my memories of my mother for weeks after that are pictures of her sitting sewing, her sweet thin face, with dark circles under the eyes, bending over the work and her fingers flying. She was making blouses for a factory. There were always piles of them, finished and unfinished, on the table and bed, and she never stopped work on them. When I awoke in the night I saw her in the lamplight working, and all day long she worked, barely stopping to eat. When she had a great pile of them finished I took them to the factory and brought back more for her to do.

I used to climb the long dark stairs to the factory loft with the bundle and watch the man who took the blouses and examined them, hating him. He was a sleek fat man, with rings on his fingers, and he used to point out every stitch which was not just right, and claim there were spots on the blouses, though there were none at all, and then he kept out some of the money. My mother got half a crown—about fifty cents—for a dozen blouses, and by working all week without stopping a minute she earned about five shillings.

I would keep out three and six for the rent money, and then go bargaining at the market stalls for food. A pound of two-penny bits of meat, with a pennyworth of pot-herbs, made us a stew, and sometimes I got a bit of stale bread besides. Then I came panting up the stairs to my mother with the bundles, and gave her the rent money, warm from being clutched in my hand, and she would laugh and kiss me and say how well I had done.

The stew had to last us the week, and I know now that often my mother made only a pretense of eating, so that there would be more for me. I was always hungry in those days and used to dream of cakes and buns, but we were very happy together. Sometimes I would do an errand for some one and

27

get a penny, and then I proudly brought it to her and we would have buns, or even a herring, for supper. But she was uneasy when I was away, and wanted me to sit by her and read aloud while she worked, so I did not often leave her.

At this time she was passionately eager to have me study. She had taught me to read before, and now while she sewed she talked to me about history and other countries and peoples, and showed me how to draw maps of the world, and we played little spelling games. She had me read the Bible aloud to her for hours at a time. It was the only book we had. But most of all she taught me acting. I had a great gift for mimicry, and she had me mimic every one I saw in the streets.[1] I loved it and used to make up little plays and act them for her.

Remembering the first time I had danced on the stage, and the money I made, I wanted to go back to the music-halls, but she roused almost into a fury at the idea. All her most painful memories were of the music-hall life, and she passionately made me promise never to act in one. I could not have done it in any case, because at this time there was a law forbidding children under fourteen to work on the stage.[2] I was only eleven.

My mother grew thinner and more tired. She complained sometimes of a pain in her head, and her beautiful hair, like long, fine silk, had threads in it that shone like silver. I loved to watch them when she brushed it at night. But she was always gay and sweet with me, and I adored her. I had no life at all separate from her; all my dreams and hopes were of making her happy and buying her beautiful things, and taking her to a place in the country where she could rest and do nothing but play with me.

Then one day while I was coming from the factory with the money clutched in my hand I passed a barroom. I had never been in one, or cared to, but something seemed to attract

28

me to this one. I stood before the swinging doors, thinking with a fluttering heart of going in, and wanting to, and not wanting to, both at once. Finally I timidly pushed the doors apart and looked in. There, at a little table, drinking with some men, I saw my father.

In which I see my father for the last time; learn that real tragedy is silent; and go out into the world to make my own way.

It gave me a great shock **7** to recognize my father in the man who sat there drinking. I quivered as I looked at him. He was changed; his dark hand-some face had reddened and looked swollen and flabby; his eyes were bloodshot. He did not see me at first. The man with him appeared to be urging something, and my father cried with an oath that he would not. I caught the word "hospital," and saw his hands shake as he pounded the table. Then some one coming in pushed me into the room and he saw me.

"Hello, here's the little tike!" he cried. "Blast me, he hasn't grown an inch! Here, come here to your daddy!"

I went over to the table and stood looking at him, the bundles under my arm. He was very boisterous, calling all the men in the bar to see me, and boasting of how I could dance. He swung me to the table-top, crying, "Come, my beauty, show 'em what you can do!" and they began to clap. I danced for them, and then I mimicked them one by one until the room was in an uproar.

"He's his father's own son!" they cried. "Little Charlie Chaplin!"

My father was very proud of me and kept me at it until I was tired, and, remembering that my mother was waiting, I climbed down from the table and picked up my bundles.

"Going without a drink?" cried my father, and offered me his glass, but I pushed it away. I did not like the smell of it. My father seemed hurt and angry; he drained the glass and put it on the table with a slam, and I saw again how his hand shook.

"Just like his mother!" he said bitterly. "Despises his own

father! I'm not good enough for his little highness. She's taught him that."

"It's not true!" I cried, enraged. "My mother never says a word about you!"

"Oh, don't she?" he sneered, but his lip shook. He stared moodily at the table, drumming on it with his fingers, and then he turned to me with a dreary look in his eyes. "Well, then, come home with me," he said. "I'll take good care of you and give you a fine start in the profession and clothes that aren't rags. I can do that, yet. I'm not done for, whatever they say. Come, will you do it?"

"No," I said, "I want to stay with my mother."

"We'll see about that!" he shouted angrily. He seized my arm and shook it. "You'll come with me, if I say so. You hear?" He glared at me and I looked back at him, frightened.

"You hurt! I want to go home to my mother!" I cried.

He held me a minute and then wearily pushed me away. "All right, go and be damned!" he said. "It's a hell of a life." Then, with a sudden motion, he caught my hand and put a sovereign[1] in it. I dodged through the crowd and escaped into the street, eager to take the money to my mother.

The next week, as we were sitting together, my mother sewing and I painfully spelling out long words in my reading, the landlady came puffing up the stairs and knocked at the door.

"Your mister's took bad and in the hospital," she said to my mother. "He's sent a message 'e wants to see you."

My mother turned white and rose in a hurry to put on her bonnet, while I picked the bits of thread from her gown. Then she kissed me, told me to mind the stew and not go out till she came back, and went away.

There seemed a horror left in the room when she was gone. I could not keep my thoughts from that word "hospital," which all the poor of London fear and dread. I wandered about the room, looking from the window at the starving cats in the court and at the brick wall opposite till it grew dark. Then I ate a small plate of the stew, leaving some for my mother, and went miserably to bed.

Late in the night my mother woke me and I saw that her face was shining almost as it used to do.

"Oh, my dear!" she cried, hugging me. "It's all right. We are going to be so happy again!" She rocked back and forth, hugging me, and her hair tumbled down about us. Then she told me that when my father was well we were all going to leave London and go far away together—to Australia. We were going to have a farm there, in the country, with cows, and I was to have milk and cream and eggs, and she would make butter, and my father would never drink again. She poured it all out, in little bursts of talk, and her warm tears fell on my face.

When at last she left me to brush out her hair she hummed a little song and smiled at herself in the tiny mirror.

"I wish my hair was all brown as it used to be," she said. "It hurt him so to see it white. I will get fat in the country. Do you remember how handsome your father was and how jolly? Oh, won't it be fun?" After she had put out the light we lay a long time in the dark talking, and she told me tales of the pleasant times they had when I was little and asked if I remembered them.

After that my mother went every day to the hospital. She did not sew any more, and she bought bunches of flowers and fruit for my father and cakes for me. At night, when she tucked me in, her face was bright with hope, and hearing her laugh, I remember how seldom she had done it lately. We were both very happy.

Then one day she came in slowly, stumbling a bit. My heart

gave a terrible leap when I saw her face—gray, with a blue look about her lips. I ran to her, frightened, and helped her to a chair. She sat there quite still, not answering me at first, and then she said in a dull voice, "He's dead. He's dead. He was dead when I got there. It can't be true. He's dead."

My father had died suddenly the night before.[2] There was some confusion about the burial arrangements. My mother seemed dazed and there was no money. People came and talked with her and she did not seem to understand them, but it seemed that the music-hall people were making the arrangements, and then that somebody objected to that and undertook them—I gathered that it was my father's sister.

Then one day my mother and I dressed very carefully and went to the funeral.[3] It was a foggy cold day, late in autumn, with drops of rain falling slowly. At one end of the grave stood a thin angular woman with her lips pressed together tight, and my mother and I stood at the other. My mother held her head proudly and did not shed a tear, but her hand in mine was cold. There were several carriages and people from the music-halls with a few flowers. When the coffin was lowered into the grave the thin hard-looking woman dropped some flowers on it. My mother looked at her and she looked at my mother coldly. We had no flowers, but my mother took from my pocket a little handkerchief of hers which she had given me—a little handerchief with an embroidered border which I prized very much—and put it in my hand.

"You can put that in," she said, and I dropped it into the open grave and watched it flutter down. My heart was almost breaking with grief for my mother.

Then we went back to our cold room alone, and my mother went at once at her sewing.

We had no more talks or study, and she did not seem to

hear when I read aloud, so after a time I stopped. She sat silently, all day, sewing at the blouses, and I hunted for errands in the streets, and made the stew, and tried to get her to eat some. She said she did not care to eat because her head ached, she would rather I had it.

At this time I looked everywhere for work, but could not seem to find any. I was so small and thin that people thought I could not do it well. I picked up a few pennies here and there and learned the ways of the streets, and wished I were bigger and not so shabby, so that I might go on the stage. I was sure I could make money there.

Then one day I came home and found my mother lying on the floor beside her chair, gray and cold, with blue lips. I could not rouse her. I screamed on the staircase for the landlady, and she came up and we worked over my mother together. After a while the parish doctor came—a busy bustling little man. He pursed up his lips and shook his head. "Infirmary case!" he said briskly. "Looks bad!"

A wagon came and they took my mother away, still gray and cold. She had not moved or spoken to me. When she had gone I sat at the top of the staircase in blank hopeless misery, thinking of the grave in which they had buried my father, and that I would never see my mother again. After a while the landlady came up with a broom.

"Well, well," she said crossly. "I 'ave my room to let again. It's a 'ard world. I'm a poor woman, you know; you can't stay 'ere."

"Yes, I know. I have other lodgings," I said importantly, so that she should not see how miserable I was. I went into the room with her and looked around. I had nothing to take away but a comb and a collar. I put them in my pocket and left.

When I was on the stairs the landlady called to me from the top.

"You know I'd like to keep you 'ere if I could," she said. "Yes, I know. But I can look out for myself," I said. I put my hands in my pockets and whistled to show her I needed no pity, and went out into the street.[4]

In which I take lodgings
in a barrel and find that I have
invaded a home; learn something about crime;
and forget that I was to share in nefarious profits.

It was a cold wet evening in the beginning of winter and the rain struck chilly through my thin clothes as I walked, wondering where I could find shelter. Probably in America a homeless, hungry child of eleven would find friends, but in London I was only one of thousands as wretched as I.[1] Such poverty is so common there that people are accustomed to it and pass by with their minds full of their own concerns.

I wandered aimlessly about for a long time, watching the gas lamps flare feebly, one by one, and make long, glimmering marks on the wet pavements. I could not whistle any more, there was such an ache in my throat at the thought of my mother, and I was so miserable and forlorn. At last I found an overturned barrel with a little damp straw in it in an alley, and I curled up in it and lay there hearing the raindrops muffled, hollow, beating above me.

After a while I must have fallen into a doze, for I was awakened by something crawling into the barrel. I thought it was a dog and put out my hand, half afraid and half glad of the company. It was another boy.

"Hello, 'ere!" he said. "Wot are you up to? This 'ere is *my* 'ome!"

"I don't care, I'm here and I'm going to stay here," I said. "Say what you like about that!"

"Ho, you are, are you? I'll punch your bloomin' 'ead off first!" he answered.

"I won't go, not for twenty punchings," I said doggedly. There was not room to fight in the barrel and I was sure he could not get me out, because I knew by the feel of his wet shoulder in the dark that he was smaller than I.

"'Ere's a pretty go, a man carn't 'ave 'is own 'ome!" he said bitterly, after we had sat breathing hard for a minute. "Wot's yer name?"

I told him who I was and how I had come there and promised to leave in the morning. He was much interested in hearing that I had a mother and asked what she was like, assuming at once a condescending air. He had never had a mother, he said importantly; he knew his way about, he did.[2]

"You can stye 'ere if you like," he said grandly. "'Ave you 'ad grub?"

I told him no, that I had not been able to find anything to eat.

"Hi know, the cats get to it first," he said. "But hi 'ave my wye, hi 'ave. 'Ere's 'arf a bun for yer." He put into my hand a damp bit of bread and I ate it gratefully while he talked. His name was Snooper, he said, and he could show me about—how to snatch purses and dodge the bobbies and have larks.

At last we went to sleep, curled in the damp straw, with an understanding that the next day we should forage together for purses. Next morning I was awakened by a terrific noise, and crawling from the barrel found Snooper standing outside kicking it. He was a wizened, small child, not more than nine years old, wearing a ragged coat too small for him and a man's trousers torn off at the knee. He wore his cap on one side with a jaunty air and whistled, his hands in the rents in his coat.[3]

We started off together to Covent Garden market, where he said we would find good pickings, and seeing the knowing cock of his eye and his gay manner, I too managed to whistle and walk with a swagger, through my heart was still heavy with missing my mother, and I was very hungry. It was early when we came to the market, but the place was crowded with farmers' wagons and horses and costers' carts. We wandered about and Snooper, with great enterprise, filled the front of his blouse with raw eggs, which we ate in a nearby alley. When we returned to the market it was beginning to fill with purchasers. Snooper, with his finger at his nose and a cock of his eye, pointed out one of them, a fat woman in black, carrying a fat leather purse.

"When I glom the leather[4] you hupset the heggs at 'er feet," he said to me in a hoarse whisper, and we edged closer to her through the crowd. She was standing before a vegetable stand with a bunch of herbs in her hand arguing with the farmer.

"Thrippence," said the farmer firmly.

"Tuppence ha'penny, not a farthing more," she said. "It's robbery, that's wot it is." We edged closer.

"Worth fourpence by rights," said the farmer. "Take 'em for thrippence or leave 'em."

"Tuppence ha'penny," she insisted. "They're stale. Tuppence ha'—ow!" Snooper had snatched her purse.

With a yell she leaped after him, stumbled and fell in the crate of eggs. The farmer, rushing from behind his stand, overturned the pumpkins, which bounced among the crowd. There was great uproar. I fled.

Diving under wagons and dodging among the horses and people, I had gone half-way down the big market when I encountered a perspiring, swearing farmer, who was trying to unload his wagon and hold his horse at the same time. The beast was plunging and rearing.

"Hi, lad!" the farmer called to me. "Want a ha'penny? 'Old 'is bloomin' 'ead for me and I'll gi' you one."

I gladly seized the halter, and a few minutes later I had the halfpenny and a carrot as well. I liked the market, with all its noise and bustle and the excitement of seeing new things, and while I wandered through the crowd munching my carrot I decided to stay there. Snooper had said he would wait for me at the barrel and divide the contents of the purse, but among all the interesting sights and sounds of the market I forgot that, and although I looked for him several days later, I never saw him again.

Before noon I had earned another ha'penny and an apple, only partly spoiled. I had not eaten an apple since the old days when I was very little and mother used to bring home treats to Sydney and me. The loneliness of my mother still lay at the bottom of my heart like a dull ache, and I determined to take the apple to her. The parish doctor who had taken her away had said I might be able to see her at the hospital that afternoon.

I held the apple carefully all the long way through the London streets to the hospital. It was a big bare place, with very busy people coming and going, and for a long time I could not get any one to tell me where my mother was. At last a woman all in black, with a wide, flaring white cap on her head, took my hand and led me past a great many beds with moaning people in them to the one where my mother lay.

They had cut away all her beautiful hair, and her small bare head looked strange upon the pillow. Her eyes were wide open and bright, but they frightened me, and though she was talking rapidly to herself, she did not say a word to me when I stood beside her and showed her the apple.

"Mother, mother, see, I've brought you something," I said, but she only turned her head restlessly on the pillow.

"One more. Are the bottonholes finished? Nine more to make the dozen, and then a dozen more, and that's a half-crown, and thread costs so much," she went on to herself.

"What's the matter with my mother? Why don't she speak to me?" I asked the woman in the white cap.

"It's the fever—she's out of her head, poor thing," the woman said.

"Won't she ever be able to speak to me?" I asked her, and something in the way she shook her head and said she didn't know made me cold all over. Then she led me out again and I went back to Covent Garden market.

In which I trick a Covent Garden coster; get glorious news from Sydney; and make another sad trip to the hospital.

I slept that night in cuddled close to the back which was warm, but intervals by wheezing Covent Garden market, of a coster's donkey, caused me great alarm at loudly and making as if to turn over upon me. Then I scurried out of the straw and wandered about in the empty, echoing place, feeling very small in the vast dimness among the shadows, until the donkey was quiet again and I could creep back beside him.

In the strange eerie chill of the morning, while the gas lamps in the streets were still showing dimly through in the fog, the farmers began to come in with their wagons. I hurried about in the darkness of the market, asking each one if I might help him unload the vegetables or hold the horse for a half-penny, or even for a carrot or raw potato. The horses were large, heavy-footed beasts and their broad, huge-muscled chests towered over me as I held the halters, while every toss of their heads lifted me from the floor. But I held on bravely, very hungry, thinking of the bun I might buy with a halfpenny, and indeed, before the market was light I had two halfpennies and a small assortment of vegetables.

I ate these, and then I went out into the dirty, cobbled streets about the market where the heavy vans were already beginning to rumble by and found an eating-house where, for my penny, I bought not only two buns, but a big mug of very hot coffee as well. As I sat on a stool drinking and taking bites from the buns, the waiter leaned his elbows on the counter and asked me where I had come from and who I was.

"I am an actor," I told him, for this idea was always in the

41

back of my mind. He laughed heartily at this, and I swallowed the rest of the coffee in a hurry, scalding my throat, for I resented his laughing and wished to get away. I put the bits of bun in my pocket and slipped down from the stool, but before I had reached the door the man came around the counter with another bun in his hand.

"'Ere, me pore lad, tike this," he said kindly enough, putting the bun in my pocket. I let him do it, feeling confused and resentful, and ate the bun later, sitting on a box in the market, but I never went back to that eating-house again. I hated to be pitied.

All the months I lived in Covent Garden market I was hungry. I ate eagerly every bit of spoiled fruit or partly decayed vegetable I could find, and sometimes the farmers, amused by my dancing for them while they were eating, would give me crusts from their baskets, but my stomach was never satisfied. The people who came to Covent Garden market were poor, and halfpennies were scarce, though I hunted all day long for small jobs that I could do. Very early in the morning when the farmers first came in was the best time to find them, but sometimes days went by when all I could earn was raw vegetables.

After a time, when the market people knew me, I had permission to sleep in one of the coster's carts, with a sack over me for warmth, but at first I curled up in the straw beside the donkeys. One of the donkeys in particular was quite sleek and fat. His owner took great pride in him, feeding him every day a large portion of carrots, and fondly swearing at him while he ate them. I used to look enviously at that donkey and finally I evolved a great plan.

When the donkey had first begun to munch the carrots, I would scream from the tail of the cart, "Thieves! Thieves! Catch 'im!" and spring away, overturning boxes and making a great commotion. The coster would leave his donkey and come running, excited, and while he was wondering what had happened I would steal slyly up on the other side of the donkey and filch the carrots. The poor beast looked reproachfully at me, wagging his ears and sometimes braying frightfully, but I ran gleefully away, and sitting concealed beneath a wagon, ate his dinner for him to the last bite.

The stupid coster, amazed, would scratch his head and marvel at the donkey's appetite, but I do not remember that he ever failed to run at the cry of "Thieves!" or that I ever failed to make way with the carrots.

Several times that winter I screwed up my courage to attempt getting work on the stage, but after I had walked a long way in the foggy, dripping streets, I would be so cold and wet and so conscious of my rags and of my dirty collar that I turned back to the market again.

Sometimes at long intervals the people at the hospital let me see my mother, but I could not bear to look at her, she was so altered and seemed so strange. She lay quite still, sometimes, and would not speak or answer me when I called to her, so that I thought she was dead, and a great black misery came over me. Sometimes she turned her head from side to side on the pillow and talked to herself in a quick, clear voice about blouses, dozens and dozens of blouses. She never looked at me or seemed to know that I was there, and I came away from the hospital so wretched that I wished never to go back.

Still I went again, as often as they would let me, and one day a marvelous thing happened. The nurse with the flaring white cap took me into a little office and showed me a letter.

"A woman brought it here from the lodgings where your mother lived," she said. "We read it to your mother, but she could not understand, so we saved it for you."

She gave it to me and I read it in great excitement.

> "Dear mother," it read. "I am coming back from Africa.[1] I will be home for Christmas Day, with thirty pounds saved, and I am bringing grand presents for you, but I will not tell you what they are. Tell Charlie to look out for his big brother, I have presents for him, too. I will be home two months from to-day, at Waterloo station at nine o'clock. Be sure to have a Christmas pudding ready. Hoping you are all well, I am your dutiful son,
>
> > "Sydney.
>
> "Postscript—It is a shawl, and there are earrings, too, but I will not tell you what else."

My heart gave a great leap and seemed to choke me, and I trembled so I could not speak. I had not thought of Sydney for a long time, and now he was coming home with money and presents! And thinking of my poor mother, who was so ill and could not understand the great news, tears came into my eyes so that I had to rub them not to let the nurse see. Then I saw how dirty I was, and ragged, and was ashamed to have Sydney see me.

The nurse kindly told the day, and comparing it with the date of the letter, I saw it was that very evening that Sydney would reach London.

Quivering with excitement, I begged to see my mother again and tell her about it, and when they said I might, I could not walk down the long ward, but must run in my eagerness. "Mother! Mother! Sydney's coming home! With presents for you—a shawl, and earrings!" I cried. But it was no use. My mother lay there with her thin drawn face quite still and would not even open her eyes.

So, with a heavy heart, wondering how I was to tell Sydney of all that had occurred, I came out of the hospital and tried to make ready for going to Waterloo station.

I washed my face and hands carefully in a puddle and dried them upon some straw. Then I took some mud and blacked my shoes as well as possible, and the toe which showed so that it would not be so conspicuous. Then my hands must be washed again and my hair combed. I smoothed out my wrinkled clothes as well as I could and tucked in the torn lining of my cap so that it would not show.

All this took much time, so that it was almost dusk before I started to meet Sydney, and I ran most of the way, not to be late, hoping that I would not miss him in all the confusion of the station.

In which Sydney comes home
to find father dead, mother too ill to
recognize him and me half starved and in rags.

When at last I arrived, panting, at Waterloo station the lamps were already lighted and all the place was bright with them. There was such a noise of people coming and going and so much confusion that, used as I was to the turmoil of the market, I hardly knew where to go or what to do. Besides, the manner of these people was so different and their clothes so good that I felt more than ever ashamed of my raggedness and doubtful what Sydney would think when he saw me.

However, I was so determined not to miss him that I got up courage to ask the way to the trains and was waiting there trembling with excitement and eagerness when the nine o'clock express came in. I had not quite courage enough to run forward, but hung back a little, keeping my broken shoe with the hole in it where my toe showed behind the other and looking carefully at each man that passed in the hope that he might be Sydney.

At last I saw him. He was almost seventeen then; big, well-dressed and healthy looking as he swung along with his cap pushed back looking eagerly at every woman in sight, expecting, I knew, to see my mother. He went by me without a glance and I saw his bright clean boots and the new glove he wore on the hand that held his bag. They seemed to put such a distance between us that I let him go past, not daring to stop him. I stood there stupidly looking at his back.

Then I realized that he was going, that I was losing him,

and I ran after him and desperately touched his arm. He looked down at me impatiently.

"No, lad," he said sharply, "I will carry the bag."

He went on through the station still watching for my mother, and I followed him, ashamed to speak to him again, ragged and dirty as I was, and yet not being able to let him go. At last he gave up hope of my mother's coming to meet him and went outside, where he hailed a cab. I stood there beside him trying to speak to him and choking while the driver opened the cab door and he got in. Then I could bear it no longer. I seized the door handle and clung to it desperately.

"Oh, Sydney, don't you know me?" I cried. "I'm Charlie."

He looked at me a minute, surprised, before he recognized me. Then his face went white and he pulled me into the cab, calling to the driver to go on, anywhere.

"For God's sake, what has happened?" he asked.

"Father's dead and mother's in the parish hospital, and I haven't had anywhere to sleep or to wash," I blurted out.

Sydney did not speak for a minute. His face seemed to set and harden as I watched it, while the cab bumped over the cobbles.

"How long has this been going on?" he said at last, choking over the words.

"About three months," I said. Then I told him as much as I could, tangling it up because there was so much to say—about father's death, and how my mother had sewed, and why I was so dirty because I had no soap and had to sleep in the cart, and that I could not make mother understand that his letter had come.

"And I've been—saving my money!" he said, once, like a groan, and his hand shook. Then he became very brisk and spoke sharply to the driver, ordering him where to go.

47

I sat in the cab while he got out to see about rooms and then he came back and took me into a place that seemed as beautiful as a palace—a suite of rooms with lace curtains, and carpet, and a piano, and a fireplace. I stood on some papers and undressed, while Sydney drew the bath for me, and it seemed as unreal as a fairy tale.

"Good heavens, you're starving!" Sydney cried when he saw how thin I was, and he sent out for hot milk and biscuits. Then, leaving me happy with the hot water and soap and plenty of clean soft towels, he went out, taking my rags done in a bundle.

When he came back I was sitting wrapped in his bathrobe, curling my toes before the fire, as happy as I could possibly be. He brought new clothes for me, warm underwear and a Norfolk suit and new shoes. When I was dressed in them, with my hair combed and a bright silk tie knotted under a clean white collar, I walked up and down, feeling cocky enough to speak to a king, except when I saw Sydney's white set face and thought of my poor mother.

"I got a permit to see her to-night," Sydney said. "I have the cab waiting. I thought maybe when she saw the presents I brought—and saw you looking so well—she always liked you best—"

So we set out in the cab again for the hospital. I felt quite grand coming up the steps in my new clothes and walked among the nurses, who did not recognize me at first, with a superior air, speaking to them confidently. I led Sydney down the long ward I knew so well, holding my head high, but all my new importance left me when I saw my mother.

She lay there with her eyes closed and her sweet face so thin, with deep hollows in the cheeks and dark marks under her lashes, that the old fear hurt my heart and I trembled.

"Is she—is she alive?" I asked the nurse.

"Yes. Speak to her and rouse her if you can," she said. Sydney and I leaned over the bed and called to her.

"Mother, look! Here's Sydney home! Look, mother!" I said cheerily.

"See, mother dear—all the beautiful presents. Wake up and see—it's Christmas!" Sydney said, taking her hand. She did not seem to hear at first, and then she turned her head on the pillow and opened her eyes.

"Here we are, mother!" we cried happily. "All the hard times are over—we'll have Christmas together—look at the lovely things Sydney's brought—see Charlie's new clothes." We tumbled the words together, excited and eager.

"Is—it—morning?" mother said painfully. "Three dozen more to sew. He shouldn't keep out the money for spots, there were no spots at all. Twelve make a dozen, and that's a half-crown, and then a dozen more, and then a dozen more, and then a dozen more—" She did not know us at all.

Sydney spread over the bed the beautiful shawl he had brought for her and put the earrings in her hand and showed her the comb of brilliants for her hair, which the nurses had cut away, but she only turned her head restlessly on the pillow and talked wildly until the nurse told us we must come away.

We rode back to the rooms, not saying a word. Sydney sat with his arm about my shoulders and his eyes were hard and bright. When we were home again he ordered up a great supper of chops and a meat pie and pudding. We sat down and he piled my plate high with food. Then suddenly he put his arms down on the table and began to sob.

It was terrible. He could not stop. I tried to speak to him, but could not, so after a moment I got up and went over to the window. I stood there leaning my forehead against the glass, looking at the lights outside, so miserable that I could not cry. What was the good of all this comfort without our mother?

Sydney came over after a while and we stood together not saying anything for a long time. Then he drew a deep breath and said: "Well, all we can do is to go on. I suppose we must look up a berth for you after you have been fed up a bit. What do you want to do?"

"I want to be an actor," I answered dully.

"All right. We'll see what we can do tomorrow," he said.

**In which I vainly
make the rounds of the theatrical
agents; almost go to sea; and at last get
the chance for which I have long been yearning.**

Nothing, I believe, makes so much difference, not only with the appearance of a man, but with the man himself, as good clothes and a well-filled stomach, and this is even more true of a boy, who is more sensitive to impressions of every sort.

When I was dressed next morning in my new clothes, which already had almost ceased to feel strange to me, and had eaten a breakfast so large that Sydney's eyes widened with alarm while he watched me, I did not feel at all like the shabby boy of the day before. I did a few dance steps, in high spirits, and mimicked for Sydney's benefit a great many of the market people and the coster who had fed his donkey carrots. I even assumed a little of my old patronizing attitude toward Sydney, who had never been considered the clever one of the family, and promised him large returns for all he had done for me as soon as I should become a famous actor.

This matter of cleverness I believe now to be greatly overrated. The clever person is too apt to let his cleverness excuse the absence of most of the solid qualities of character, and to rely on facility and surface brilliance to supply the want of industry and prudence. All my life I have been going up like a rocket, all sparks and a loud noise, and coming down like one again, but Sydney has always been the steady stand-by of the family, ready to pick me out of the mud and start me up again. He is the better man of the two.

That morning, though, after I had eaten his breakfast, I could not imagine myself ever in need of help again and my mind was full of future success on the stage. I could hardly wait while he dressed to go with me to the agents, and when we were in the streets I walked with a swagger, and pointed out the sights as if he were only a provincial and I at least a capitalist of London.

I was just twelve then and the law was strict against the employment on the stage of children under fourteen, but I do not remember that I ever had any difficulty in convincing the agents that I was over the legal age. My self-confidence and my talent for mimicry were so strong that they overcame the impression of my small size, and I suppose the month of hunger and suffering for my mother had given my face an older look.

In the weeks which followed Sydney's homecoming we visited dozens of agents. I climbed the long stairs to their offices in a fever of expectation and hope; I talked to each agent quite confidently, and when he had taken my name and address and said nothing for me at present, I came down again in the depths of gloom, so despondent that only a good dinner and a visit to the theater would cheer me. I always felt that I could play the parts much better than any actor I saw, and so I came away in high spirits again.

Every day we went to see my mother, and the nurses said she was a little better, but she never knew us or spoke to us and we could not see any change. This sadness because she could not be happy with us made our rooms seem gloomy when we returned to them, and I know that Sydney felt it always. Often, planning what we should do when she was well again, and how proud she would be of my success when I was a great actor, I almost believed it all true and was as happy as if it were. My imagination has always seemed truer to me than facts.

Christmas came and went and I did not have an offer of a place on the stage. Sydney must go back to sea. Nearly all of his savings were gone and he felt he must leave some money to buy little delicacies for my mother. The problem of what to do with me bothered him, and when he spoke of it, as he did sometimes, all my dreams faded suddenly and I felt so desolate that if I had been smaller I would have wept in despair.

At last he arranged with his company to take me on the ship as a cabin-boy. He said it would not be half bad, I might grow to like the sea, and although I hated the thought of it, it seemed better than going back to Covent Garden market again. We were to sail sometime in January, bound for Africa. As a last resort we made the rounds of the theatrical agents again, but there was nothing in sight for me, and so it was settled that I must go to sea.

Sydney bought me a little bag and packed it with the things I should need on ship-board. We gave up the lodgings and paid a last visit to mother. This time she was quieter and looked at us several times almost as if she recognized us. It nearly broke my heart to leave her so, but we could not think of anything else to do.

The morning of our last day in London my breakfast almost choked me. Our bags were packed, waiting beside our chairs, and it seemed to me that everything in the world was wrong. I knew I should not like the sea. The maid had brought in a few letters, with the bill for the lodgings, and Sydney was looking them over. Suddenly he looked at me queerly and threw a card across the table to me.

"Seems to be for you," he said. I turned it over in a hurry and read it. It said, "Call and see me, Frank Stern, 55 the Strand." Frank Stern was a theatrical agent.

I leaped from my chair with a shout of excitement.

"What price the sea now?" I cried. "I've got a place worth the whole of it! Where's my hat?"

"Go slow, go slow, lad," said Sydney. "You haven't got the place yet, you know."

"I've as good as got it," I retorted, tearing open the bags to find my comb and a clothes brush. "Come, now, Sydney, lend me your cane? An actor has to have a cane you know."

Sydney lent me his cane, and I leaped down the stairs three steps at a time.

A tram would not do, I must have a cab to go in a style suiting my new position. All the way I gave myself the airs of a great actor, looking haughtily from the cab-window at the common Londoners and thinking how the audiences would applaud when I strode down the stage.

Frank Stern was a little man, plump and important, with a big diamond on his finger, and he began by clearing his throat in an impressive manner and looking me over very sharply, but I sat down with a careless air, swinging Sydney's cane and asked him in an offhand way if he had anything particularly good. At the moment so great was the power of my imaginings on my own mind I felt quite careless as to whether I got the place or not and was resolved not to take any small part unworthy my talents.

"It's the leading part with a provincial company *From Rags to Riches*,"[1] he said. "Our lead's fallen sick and we need a new one in a hurry. Think you can do it?"

"E—Er—provincial company," I said doubtfully. "I had not thought of leaving London. Still—what's the screw?"[2]

"One pound ten a week," he answered.

"Impossible!" I said. "I could not think of it."

"Well—we might make it two pounds. We need some one in a hurry. If you are a quick study and make a good showing at rehearsal—say two pounds. Yes, I'll make it two pounds."

"It's a small salary—a very small salary," I said gruffly. I, who had been glad to steal a donkey's carrots only a few weeks earlier! But I did not think of that. I thought of my great talents, wasted in a provincial company. "I'll think it over," I told the agent, seeing he would not increase the amount.

"No. I must know right now," he replied firmly.

I wrinkled my brows with an air of indecision and thought for a minute.

"All right, I'll do it," I said.

"Rehearsal to-morrow at ten," Frank Stern said, giving me the address in a quite commonplace manner.

**In which I rehearse
the part of the boy hero of the
thrilling melodrama, *From Rags to
Riches;* and start off on a tour of the provinces.**

I saw Sydney off on **12** the ship for Africa, having induced him to give me the cane, and as I stood waving at him I was so elated with success that I felt almost intoxicated. I was an actor at last—a real actor, with a rehearsal in prospect! I strutted up and down on the dock a bit after Sydney was gone feeling sorry for all the people about, who little realized what an important person they were passing so heedlessly. Then I took a cab again, as due to my position, and gave the driver the address of the rooms Sydney had taken for me in Burton Crescent.[1]

I was not only an actor, but a man with an income of my own and bachelor chambers. I was very haughty with the charwoman who brought in the coals for my fire, and I sat frowning for some time in an attitude of deep thought, pondering whether I should have cream tart or apple-and-blackberry pudding for dinner. At last I decided on both and ate them in state before my own fire. It was a great evening.

Next morning I was divided between my eagerness to hurry to the rehearsal and my feeling that it would more accord with my importance if I should arrive a little late. It was not until the cab began to rattle over the cobbles about Covent Garden market that a sense of strangeness began to come over me, and I realized that I had never acted before and should not quite know what to do at the rehearsal. I looked from the windows of the cab at the costers' donkeys and thought what a short time ago I had envied them, woebegone and hungry as they were.

The rehearsal was in a room over a public house in Covent

Garden, and as I climbed the stairs I began to feel small and a bit uncertain. When I went in the room was full of people standing about or sitting on boxes, and they all looked at me with interest. At one end, near the rough stage, was a little table with three important-looking men standing beside it, and after a look around I walked up to them.

"I am Charles Chaplin," I said, wishing I were taller. "I am, I believe, to play leading man in your production."

They looked me over as Mr. Stern had done, rather sharply, and then introduced themselves. The man in the dirty plaid waistcoat was Joe Baxter, manager of *From Rags to Riches*, and also the villain in the piece. The company had been playing for a ten weeks' round of the suburbs and was now about to go into the provinces. They were already delayed by the illness of the lead, which Mr. Baxter cursed roundly, and his chief interest in me was the hope that I was a quick study. I assured him that I was, and without any further talk he began to read the play to me.

It appeared that I was to play the boy hero, an earl's son, defrauded of my rights by the villain after my mother had pitifully died in the streets of London with property snow sifted on her from the flies. I wandered in rags through three acts, which contained a couple of murders, a dozen hair-breadth escapes, and comic relief by the comedian, and I came triumphantly into my own in the fourth act, where the villain died a terrible death.

Now whether my liking for mimicry came to my aid or whether my own experiences, so much like those of the part I was to play, had given me material which I used unconsciously, I do not know, but when Mr. Baxter gave me my part and asked me to read it, I did it well. Mr. Baxter stood chewing his cigar when I had finished, and the look on his face was less discontented.

"Orl right," he said briskly. "Now, ladies and gents, ready!

57

First act, second scene, Lord Plympton's droring-room! You walk through this and read your part," he said to me. "No time for study, got to play Sweetbay[2] to-morrow night. Do the best you can with it."

The woman who was to play my mother came over while I stood waiting with the part in my hand. She was a thin sallow woman in a bright red waist and a hat with blue and yellow feathers.

"Have a toffy?" she said, holding out a bag.

"No, thanks. I left off eating them years ago," I answered, swinging my cane.

"Horrid play, aren't it?" she went on. "Beastly life, on tour. How do you like your part?"

"Oh," I answered carelessly, "it's not much of a part, but I do what I can with it. I won't mind the provinces for a season. I'm tired of London."

"Here you, Reginald—Chaplett, whatever your name is— come on!" Mr. Baxter yelled, and I started forward on to the stage. Mr. Baxter uttered such a sound, between a groan and a roar, that I stopped, startled.

"Good Gawd!" he moaned. "That's the window, you idiot! Come through the door! Come through the door! What do you think you are, a bloomin' bird?"

It was hard work, rehearsing on the bare stage, with no idea what the scenery was to be, and Mr. Baxter went from rage to profanity and from that to speechlessness and groans while he drove us through the parts. We worked all day and late into the night and he did not let me stop a minute, although I grew hungry and the smell of the fried fish the other actors ate while I was on the stage took my mind from the work. At last he let me go, with a groan.

"It couldn't well be worse!" he said grimly. "Now, ladies and gents, Waterloo station eleven sharp to-morrow, ready fer Sweetbay!"

CHARLIE CHAPLIN'S OWN STORY

I came very wearily down the flight of stairs holding the bundle of manuscript and my cane while the words of my part and all the stage directions buzzed together in my brain. I had not money enough for a cab; if we were to go to Sweetbay the next day I must walk back to my rooms. It was a cold foggy night and my steps sounded loud and echoing on the pavements as I hurried along, tired and hungry, almost ready to wish for a coster's cart that I might crawl into and rest. But I held as firmly as I could to the thought that I was an actor, though finding small comfort in it, and when at last I had reached my rooms I had persuaded myself that I was driven by the duties and ambitions of a great position. So I scowled fiercely at my reflection in the mirror over the mantel, and tying a towel about my head so as to look the character of a diligent student, I sat all night reading the words of my part and committing them to memory.

Next morning, when I reached the station with my bag, the rest of the company was waiting, very draggled and weary looking, while Mr. Baxter bustled about, swearing loudly. My spirits rose at the noise and excitement of the starting, and when I saw the compartment labeled, "Reserved: *From Rags to Riches* company," I held my head proudly again, hoping that passers-by would notice and say to each other, "See! He must be the leading man."

I lingered on the platform until the last minute, looking as important as I could and thinking how well the cane carried out the effect, and then, as the engine began to puff and the train slowly started, I swung myself aboard and walked into the compartment where the company was settling itself for the trip to Sweetbay.

**In which I encounter the
difficulties of a make-up box; make
my first appearance in drama; and learn
the emptiness of success with no one to share it.**

The rest of the **13** company were very
glum on that journey to Sweetbay, sitting
hunched up any way in their seats and
looking drearily from the windows, not
even glancing a me as I strode up and down the compartment,
murmuring the words of my part to myself and hoping Mr.
Baxter was noticing how studious I was.

"Well enough for you, old man," I said to myself, seeing
him absorbed in a copy of *Floats*[1] and not even looking in my
direction. "Wait till you see me act!" But I felt my spirits somewhat dampened by his indifference, nevertheless.

When the train stopped at Sweetbay I stepped to the platform with a lively air and stood looking around while the others dragged down the steps. It was raining a little, very few
people were about and they were not at all interested in us,
which seemed to me a personal affront.

"Hustle, now! No time to look for lodgings till after
matinée!" Mr. Baxter said briefly, and set off at a brisk pace,
the rest of us straggling behind him through the streets.

I walked as jauntily as possible, swinging my cane with an
air, but the gloom of it all depressed me. I wished myself older
than twelve years, and larger, so that I would not have to look
up at the others, and I wondered if I could do the make-up
right, but determined not to ask any one how it was done. I had
bought a make-up box and experimented a bit before my mirror, but I was doubtful of the effect on the stage.

When we reached the Theater Royal, a dark smelly place,
with littered, dirty dressing-rooms, I felt quite helpless before

the problem. It appeared that all the men were to share one dressing-room, and I crowded into the tiny place with the others and opened my make-up box, ashamed of its new look. The comedian and Lord Plympton, who behind the scenes was a sallow gloomy individual with a breath smelling of beer and onions, sat down at once in their shirt-sleeves before the small cracked mirrors and bagan smearing their faces with grease-paint, for we were late, and already the lights had gone on in front and a few people were shuffling in.

I made shift with the make-up as best I might and hurried into the ragged suit I was to wear in the first scene, pinning it up in small folds about me, for it was the costume worn by the former lead and too large for me. However, I hoped to make it do, and when, by the glimpses I could get of myself in the mirror, it seemed to be all right, I left the dressing-room and wandered into the wings, feeling well satisfied with myself.

The stage was shadowy and dark behind the big canvas scenes. "A street in a London slum" was already set, and the scene shifters, swearing in hoarse whispers, were wheeling Lord Plympton's drawing-room into position for a quick change. I made my way warily around this and encountered Mr. Baxter, who was rushing about in a frenzy, roundly cursing everything in sight. When he saw me he stopped short.

"Good Gord!" he cried. "Going on like this?"

"What's wrong?" I asked, startled.

"Wrong? Wrong? Why was I ever a manager?" moaned Mr. Baxter, seizing his head in both hands. "You gory idiot!" he exploded, and seemed to choke.

"What's the row, Joe?" the woman who was to play my mother asked, coming over to us, while I stood very uneasy and doubtful what to say.

"Look at 'im!" roared Mr. Baxter. "How many times have I told him he's pathetic—PATHETIC! And here he comes with a face like a bloomin' cranberry! And he goes on in six minutes!"

"I'll look out for the lad," the woman said, kindly enough, and taking me by the hand she led me into the women's dressing-room, where she made up my face with her own paint and powder and I squirmed with humiliation.

"It's your first shop, aren't it?" she said, drawing the dark circles under my eyes, and I drew myself up with as much dignity as possible in the circumstances and said stiffly, "This is my first engagement with a provincial company."

Then I returned to the wings and waited with beating heart for my cue. Mr. Baxter, made up as the villain now, stood beside me giving me last orders, but my head whirled so I could hardly hear him, and all the lights made a dazzling glare in my eyes. Then my cue came—my mother, on the stage, moaned piteously, and Mr. Baxter gave me a little push. I stumbled out on the stage, crying, "See, mother dear, here is a crust!"

The blinding glare in my eyes and the confusion in my brain were over in a minute. The strangeness of it all fell away from me, and, in a manner I can not explain to one who is not an actor, I was at the same time the ragged, hungry child, starving in Covent Garden market, and the self-conscious actor playing a part. I wept sincerely for the suffering of my poor mother, who moaned at my feet, and at the same time I said to myself, proudly, "What, ho! *now* they see how pathetic I am, what?" When I did not remember the words I made them up, paying no heed to the villain's anxious prompting behind his hand, and I defied him vigorously at the close of the act, crying, "You shall touch my mother only over my dead body!" with enthusiasm. The curtain fell and there was a burst of applause behind it.

"Not half bad, what?" I said triumphantly to Mr. Baxter, while my stage mother scrambled to her feet, and he replied moodily, "Don't be so cocky, young 'un. There's three acts yet to go."

But I was warmed up to the work now and I enjoyed it, wandering forlorn through my imitation griefs and at last coming grandly into my rights as the earl's son and wearing the splendor of the velvet suit with great aplomb in the last act, although I was obliged surreptitiously to hold up the trousers with one hand because I could not find enough pins in the dressing-room to make them fit me. I felt that I was the hit of the piece and rushed out of the theater afterward to find lodgings and eat a chop before the evening performance with all the emotions of an actor who had arrived at the pinnacle of fame. I could not forbear telling the waiter who served me the chop, at a grimy little eating house not far from the theater, that I was the leading man of the *From Rags to Riches* company and must be served quickly, as pressing duties awaited me at the theater before the evening performance. He looked down at me with a broad grin on his fat face and said, "You don't say, now!" in a highly gratifying tone, although I wished he had said it more solemnly.

That night, sitting alone in my bed-sitting-room in actors' lodgings, I was greatly pleased with myself and wished only that my mother were there to see me. I wrote her a long letter, telling her how well I had done and promised to send her at least ten shillings, and perhaps a pound, when I was paid on Saturday. Then I went out into the dark silent streets where the rain fell mournfully to post it. The night was very gloomy. After all, I was only twelve and had no friends anywhere except Sydney, who had gone to Africa. I thought of my mother lying alone in the hospital and perhaps not able to understand my glad news when it should arrive, and such a feeling of sadness and loneliness came over me that I hurried back to my room and crawled into bed without lighting the gas, very unhappy, indeed.

In which I taste the flavor of success; get unexpected word from my mother; and face new responsibilities.

However, though I never entirely forgot my mother in **14** London, I enjoyed the life on tour with the *From Rags to Riches* company, with all the excitement of catching trains and finding different lodgings in each town, and I never understood the grumblings of the others when we traveled all night and had to rush to a matinée without resting. I liked it all; I liked the thrill of having to pause in a scene while the audience applauded, as they did pretty often after I became used to the stage. I liked standing with the others after the Saturday matinée, when Mr. Baxter came around giving each one his salary, and I had great fun afterward jingling the two pounds in my pocket and feeling very wealthy and important when I spent sixpence for a copy of *Floats*.

Best of all I liked lying late in bed Sunday mornings, as I could do sometimes, and looking for my name in the provincial journals—"Charles Chaplin, as Reginald, showed an artistic appreciation which gives promise of a brilliant future," or "Charles Chaplin, the talented young actor, plays the part of Reginald with feeling."

Then, though no one could see me, I would pretend great indifference, yawning wearily and saying: "Oh, very well for a provincial journal, but wait till we get to London!" But I always saved the clippings.

I became friendly with the comedian, who was a fat good-humored fellow enough, and always got a laugh in the third act by sitting on an egg. I sometimes treated him to oysters after the show on Saturday nights, and he used to grumble about the stage, saying: "It's a rotten life, lad, a rotten life. You'd be well out of it." Then he would shake his head mournfully and stop a great sigh by popping an oyster into his mouth.

"It suits me, old top," I would reply, with a wave of my hand, thinking that when I was his age I would have London at my feet.

I did not care much for the others in the company, as I felt they greatly underrated my importance, and I especially shunned Cora, the woman who played my mother, because she was inclined to make a small boy of me behind the scenes, and would inquire if my socks were darned or if my underwear were warm, no matter who was present.

In the spring the tour of *From Rags to Riches* came to an end. For the last time I clutched my stage mother while the paper snow was sifted on us from the flies; for the last time I defied the villain and escaped the murderer and wore the velvet suit, very shabby now, but fitting better, when I came back to Lord Plympton's drawing-room.

I felt very depressed and lonely when I came off the stage. The company was breaking up, most of them were gone already, and the "Street in a London Slum" had been loaded into a wagon with "The Thieves' Den" and "The Thames at Midnight." No one was in sight but the grubby scene shifters, who were swearing while they struggled with Lord Plympton's drawing-room, and the dressing-room was deserted by all but the comedian, who was very drunk, and said mournfully: "It's a rotten life, it's a rotten life."

I dressed quickly and went back to my lodgings, wondering with a sinking heart what I should do next. I had seen enough of stage life by that time to realize that it was not easy to get a hearing on the Strand,[1] and for the first time I took small comfort in the thought of my pile of clippings from the provincial journals. My rooms were cold and dark, but no gloomier than my mood when I went in, hunting in my pockets for a match to light the gas.

When the gas flared up I saw a letter propped against the cold pasty set out for my supper. I took it up, surprised, for it was the first letter I had ever received, and then I saw on the envelope the name of the parish hospital where I had left my mother.

I tore it open quickly, but my hands were shaking so it seemed a long time before I could get the sheet of paper out of the envelope. I held it close to the gas and read it. It said that my mother had asked them to write and say she was glad I was doing so well. She was able to leave the hospital now if I could take her away, or should they send her to the almshouse, as she was not strong enough to work?

I could not eat or sleep that night. Some time about dawn the landlady came knocking at my door and spoke bitterly through the panels about my wasting her gas, threatening to charge it extra on the bill. I said I was packing, paid her for the lodging, and told her to go away. Then I went out with my bags, in a very dark and chilly morning, when the early carts were beginning to rattle through the empty streets. I rode up to London on the first train, my mind torn between joy and a sort of panic, confused with a dozen plans, all of which seemed valueless.

My mother was sitting up in bed with Sydney's shawl wrapped about her when I was allowed to see her. Her hair was longer and curled about her face, but there were dark circles under her eyes and she looked very little, almost like a child.

"My, my, what a great lad you've grown!" she said, and then she began to cry. The least excitement made her sob, and her hands trembled all the while I was there.

"Never you mind, mother; I'll take care of you!" I said briskly, and I told her what a great success I had become on the stage. It was the first pose I had ever taken which did not deceive myself, for I wondered, miserably while I talked, what we should do if I could get no engagement. I promised to take her soon to beautiful lodgings, and the words sounded hollow to me as I said them, but she seemed pleased and was greatly cheered when I left her. Without stopping to look for lodgings for myself, I hurried at once to the Strand, eager to see the agents.

Now in the success or failure of an actor a great deal depends on luck, as I was very willing to admit later when it turned against me, although in the early days I ascribed all my good fortune to my own great merit. On that day when I walked down the Strand I passed dozens of actors who had been struggling for years to find a foothold on the stage, going from one small part to another, with months of starvation between, furbishing up their shabby clothes and walking endless miles up and down the stairs to the agents' offices in vain. The numbers of them appalled me. Frank Stern's outer office was full of them and they did not leave off watching his door with hungry eyes to look at me when I walked in and gave my card to the office boy.

"Can't see you," he said briefly, without looking at it. "No use the rest of you waiting, either," he said raising his voice. "He won't see nobody else to-day."

They rose and began to straggle out, some of them protesting with the office boy, who only looked at them contemptuously, repeating, "He won't see nobody." I was following them when Frank Stern's door opened and he appeared.

"Oh, hello, my lad!" he said genially. "You're just the chap I want to see. Come in, come in!" He ushered me into his inner office, clapping me on the shoulder.[3]

In which I understand
why other people fall; burn my bridges
behind me; and receive a momentous telegram.

This time I sat in with no inflated importance, only fast-beating heart, **15** Frank Stern's office opinion of my own hoping, with a that he would offer me some place with salary. I could hardly hear what he said for thinking of the few coins in my pocket and my mother in the hospital waiting for me to come back and take her to the beautiful lodgings I had promised to engage.

"Joe Baxter tells me you did fairly well on tour," the agent said, after an idle remark or two. "He's taking out *Jim, the Romance of a Cockney*[1] in a few weeks. How would you like the lead?"

"I'd like it," I said eagerly, and realized the next minute I had done myself out of a raise in the pay by not asking first how much it would be. But the relief of having a part was so great that I did not much care.

I came whistling down the stairs after I had left Frank Stern, and in the Strand I looked with a different eye on the actors I passed, beginning to think that, after all, they must lack real merit such as I had, or else they drank or were not willing to work. I saw the comedian from the *From Rags to Riches* company, looking very seedy, and was passing him with a nod when he stopped me.

"How's tricks?" he asked of me. "Shopped yet?"

"Oh, yes, I have an engagement," I replied carelessly, swinging my cane. "Only a provincial company, but not so bad."

"I say, not really?" he said, surprised. "You're in luck. Look here, old chap, could you lend me five bob?"

"Well, no," I answered. "No, I'm afraid not. But I hope you're shopped soon. You ought to quit drinking, you know—you'd do better."

"Well enough for you to talk, my lad. You'll think different when you've been tramping the Strand for twenty years, like I have, and never a decent chance in the whole of them. You're on top now, but you'll find it's not all beer and skittles before you've done. I say, make it three bob—or two?"

I gave him a shilling and he begged me to say a word to Baxter for him, which I meant to do, but later forgot. Then I went searching lodgings for my mother. I found them in a private home for convalescents in Burton Crescent—very decent rooms with a little balcony overlooking a small park, and Mrs. Dobbs, the landlady, seemed a pleasant person and promised to look out for my mother while I was on tour.

My mother was delighted when she saw the place, laughing and crying at the same time, while I wrapped her in Sydney's shawl and made her comfortable with some cushions on the couch before the fire. We had tea together very cozily, and I told her I should soon be a great London actor, which she firmly believed, only saying I was too modest and made a mistake in going on tour when I should have at least a good part in a West End theater.

By closest economy I managed to send her a pound every week during that season with *Jim, the Romance of a Cockney*, though sometimes going without supper to buy the envelope and stamp; and because it is not poverty, but economy, which teaches the value of a penny, I learned it so thoroughly that year that I have never forgotten it. The only part of the tour which I enjoyed was the time I spent on the stage, when I forgot my constant thought of money and lived the romantic joys and griefs of Jim. I played the part so well, perhaps for this reason, that I was becoming known as one of the most promising boy actors in England, and I used to clip every mention of my acting which I could find and send it to my mother in the Saturday letter.

When I came back to London at the close of the season I expected nothing less than a rush of managers to engage me. I walked into Frank Stern's office very chesty and important with not even a glance for the office boy or the crowd of actors patiently waiting and knocked on his door with my cane. Then I pushed it open and went in.

Frank Stern was sitting with his feet on his desk, smoking and reading *Floats* in great contentment. He leaped to his feet when he heard me walk in, but when he saw who it was he welcomed me boisterously.

"Glad to see you back, glad to see you!" he said jovially. "Sit down."

"No, thanks. I just dropped in to see what you had to offer for next season," I said carelessly. "It must be something good this time, you know."

His cordiality dropped like a mask; he looked at me very sternly.

"There's a part in *"His Mother Left Him to Starve,"* he said. "We could use you in that."

"How much salary?" I asked.

"Two pounds," he answered sharply.

"No, thanks," I said airily. "Though I won't say I mightn't consider it for four."

"Then I'm afraid I haven't anything," he said, and turned back to his desk as though he was very busy. I went out whistling, so sure of my value that I was careless of offending him. And indeed when, ten days later, I was offered the part of Billy, the page, in *Sherlock Holmes*,[2] at a salary of thirty shillings, I was sure that I had acted astutely, and gave myself credit for good business sense as well as great talent. I even had some thoughts of holding out for a part in the London company, and if I had had a few shillings more, or any money to pay for my mother's lodgings, I might have been foolish enough to do it.

As it was, I walked into the rooms where the company was rehearsing with a feeling that it was a condescension on my part to go on tour again, and marching briskly up to the prompter's table, laid my cane upon it—a breach of theatrical etiquette at which the company stood aghast. I never did it again, for that day's work with a real stage manager gave me my first idea of good acting, and I left late that night with my vanity smarting painfully.

"'Act natural!'" I said to myself, bitterly mocking the stage manager. "'Talk like a human being!' My eye, what do they think the people want? I act like an actor, I talk like an actor, and if they don't like it they can jolly well take their old show! I can get better!"

Nevertheless, I went back next day and worked furiously under the scathing sarcasm and angry oaths of the manager until I had learned the part passably well and forgotten most of the stage tricks I had found so effective in *From Rags to Riches*. The night before we went on tour I had dinner with my mother, who was still in the care of Mrs. Dobbs, so thin and nervous that it worried me to see her, and she was fluttering with excitement and overjoyed at my being a great actor, but for the first time I doubted it.

However, the press notices speedily brought back my self-confidence. In almost every town they praised my work so highly that the actor who played Holmes gave me cold glances whenever he saw me and even cut bits of my part. Then, though complaining bitterly, I knew I had really "arrived," and I openly grinned at him before the company, and demanded a better dressing-room.

Just before the close of the tour I was standing in the wings one evening confiding to one of the actresses my intention of placing a bent pin in Holmes' chair on the stage next evening, where I calculated it would have great effect, owing to his drawing his dressing gown tight around him with a dignified air just before sitting down, when a boy came up and gave me a telegram. I tore it open, fearing bad news from my mother, and read it. It said:

"William Gillette opens in *Sherlock Holmes* here next week. Wants you for Billy. Charles Frohman."

William Gillette![3] Charles Frohman![4]

In which I journey to London;
meet and speak with a wax-works figure;
and make my first appearance in a great theater.

I do not know how I **16** got through my act
that night. I was in such a flurry of excitement and so jubilant over the
great news that I missed my cues and
played with only half my wits on my work, careless how Holmes
frowned at me. Every one in the company had heard of my
telegram from Frohman before the end of the second act, and
I knew they were watching me enviously from the wings. I
rushed past them, in wild haste to get to the dressing-room and
take off my make-up as soon as my last scene was finished, and
I was half dressed while they were taking the curtain call.

I met Holmes and the manager just outside the dressing-
room and resigned my place in their company with great
haughtiness.

"Of course—er—you understand that I—er—can not do
justice to my art as long as I am supported by merely provincial
actors," I said, looking at Holmes as majestically as I might
from a height two feet less than his. Then I drew the manager
aside and said kindly, "Of course, old man, I appreciate all
you've done, and all that—any time I can do anything for you
with Frohman, you understand, you've only to say the word."

The entire company, excepting only Holmes, was at the
station to see me off next morning, and since in the meantime
my first vainglory had diminished and I felt more my usual
self, there was a jolly half-hour before the train left. Every one
wished me luck and promised to come to see me act in London,
while I assured them I would not forget old friends, and the
manager clapped me heartily on the back and said he'd always

known I would do great things. They gave a great cheer when the train started and I waved at them from the back platform. Then I was off, to London and fame.

Early the next afternoon, dressed in a new suit with new shirt and tie to match, I arrived at the Duke of York's Theater in the West End and inquired for the stage manager. I had to wait for him a minute on the dim stage and I stood looking out over the rows of empty seats in the big dark house, thrilling to think that before long they would be filled with scores of persons watching me act. Then Mr. Postham came hurrying up, a very busy man with a quick nervous voice. I told him who I was, and he gave me the manuscript of my part in a hurried manner.

"That's all. Rehearsal here, nine to-morrow," he said. Then, as I was turning away, he added, "Like to see Mr. Gillette?"

"I would, yes," I answered eagerly, and tried to clutch at my self-possession, which I had never lacked before, while the boy led me through the dim passages to Mr. Gillette's dressing-room. The boy knocked at the door of it, said loudly, "Mr. Chaplin to see Mr. Gillette," and left me standing there, breathing hard.

An instant later the door opened and a little Japanese, perfectly dressed in the clothes of an English man-servant, popped into the aperture. I had never seen a Japanese servant[1] before, and his appearance so confounded me that I could only look at him and repeat what the boy had said, while I fumbled in my pocket for a card and wondered if it would be proper to give it to him if I should find one. It appeared that it was not necessary, for he opened the door wider. I stepped in.

William Gillette was sitting before his dressing-table, busy with make-up. He rose to meet me—a very tall stately man, his face entirely covered with dead white paint. The whole place was white—the walls, the dressing-table, even the floor, as I remember it—and the whiteness was intensified by a glare of strong white light. In that bright glare, and under the mask of white paint, Mr. Gillette did not seem like a real man. He seemed like some fantastic curio in a glass case.

"You're to play Billy,[2] I understand," he said, looking keenly at me through narrow, almost almond, eyes. "How old are you?"

"Fourteen, sir," I answered as if hypnotized, for I was now telling every one that I was sixteen.

"I hear you're a very promising young actor," he said. "I hope you'll make a good Billy—what did you want to see me about?"

"I just wanted to see you," I replied

"Well, I'm very glad we've met," he said, looking amused, I thought. "If I can be any help to you, come again, won't you?"

I think I replied suitably as I backed out. I reached the street before I quite recovered from the effect of his strange appearance in that white room. I had met one of the greatest actors on the English stage, and I felt as though I had seen a figure in a wax-works and it had spoken to me.

Then, when I stood on the curb in all the noise of the London traffic, I realized that the events of that momentous day were all real. I was engaged to play with William Gillette in the finest of West End theaters; I held the manuscript of my part in my hand. Excited and jubilant, I rushed off to tell my mother the great news, and then to engage lodgings of my own, where I spent all that evening walking up and down, rehearsing the part of Billy, only pausing now and then, with a whoop, to do a few dance steps or stand on my head.

The next morning I was one of the first to reach the theater for rehearsal. I had risen early to take a few turns up and down the Strand, hoping to meet some one I knew to whom I could mention casually that I was with Frohman now, but every one I passed was a stranger and I had to content myself with looking haughtily at them and saying to myself: "*You* wouldn't half like to be on your way to rehearsal with William Gillette, would you now? What, ho!"

Mr. Postham[3] proved to be different from the stage manager I had known before. He was nervous and excitable, but no matter how badly an actor read his lines, Mr. Postham never swore at him.

"No," he said quietly. "*This* way, 'I'll do it, sir.' No, not 'I'll do *it* sir,' but 'I'll *do* it, sir.' Try it again. No, that's a little too emphatic. Listen, 'I'll do it, sir.' Not quite so self-confident. Again, 'I'll do it, sir.' Once more, please." He never seemed to grow tired. He kept us at it for hours, watching every detail, every inflection or shade of tone, and his patience was endless. It was new work to me, but I liked it; and after rehearsal I would practise for hours in my rooms, liking the sound of my voice in the different tones.

William Gillette had come to London with a play called *Clarice*,[4] which had not gone well. He was putting on *Sherlock Holmes* to save the season and rushing rehearsals in order to have the new play ready in the shortest possible time. We worked all day, and twice were called for midnight rehearsals, after *Clarice* was off the boards. Two weeks after I reached London we were called at seven in the morning for formal dress rehearsal. *Sherlock Holmes* was to be put on that night.

Everything went wrong at the dress rehearsal. We were overworked and nervous; we missed our cues; some of the properties were lost; Mr. Postham was intensely quiet. I was very well pleased by it all, for every East End actor knows that a bad dress rehearsal means a good first performance, but the manager and Mr. Gillette did not seem to share my opinion, and the company scattered gloomily enough when at last they let us go, with admonitions to be early at the theater that night.

I was made up and dressed for the first scene early, and hurried out to the peep-hole in the curtain, hoping to catch a glimpse of my mother in the audience. I had got tickets for her and Mrs. Dobbs and ordered a carriage for them, as my mother was not strong and could not come in a tram. The house was filling fast. Behind the scenes there was tense breathless excitement; scene shifters and stage carpenters were hurrying back and forth; there was a furious scene over something mislaid. Every one's nerves were strained to the breaking point.

The curtain went up. From the wings, where I stood waiting for my cue and saying my lines over and over to myself with a tight feeling in my throat, I saw Mr. Gillette opening the scene. I listened carefully to every word he spoke, knowing that every one brought my entrance nearer. Suddenly Mr. Postham touched my shoulder.

"Royalty's in front," he said. "Whatever you do, don't look at the royal box."

Then, on the stage, Mr. Gillette spoke my cue. I put back my shoulders, cleared my throat, and stepped out on the stage, my brain repeating, "Don't look at the royal box."

In which I play with a celebrated actor; dare to look at the royal box; pay a penalty for my awful crime; gain favor with the public; and receive a summons from another famous star.

My nerves were badly tuned violin to feel them vibrate the stage and spoke **17** stretched tight, like strings, and I seemed when I stepped on my opening line, with Gillette's eyes upon me and the packed house listening. My brain was keyed to a high pitch, working smoothly, but it did not seem in any way attached to my body, and I heard the words as though some one else had spoken them. They were clear, firm, the accent perfect. I felt myself stepping three steps forward, one to the right, and turning to Mr. Gillette; heard my second line spoken, with the emphasis placed properly on the third word.

"Don't look at the royal box," I said to myself.

Then I was in the swing of the scene. Mr Gillette spoke; I answered him; the situation came clearly into my mind. I realized that I was playing opposite William Gillette, that the eyes of London were on me, and royalty itself listening. I threw myself into the work, quivering with the strain of it, but determined to play up to the big moment. I was doing well. I knew it. I saw it in the relaxation of Mr. Gillette's anxious watching. He was abandoning himself to his part, trusting me to play up to him.

"Now, Billy, listen to me carefully," he said. I turned my head to the right angle, felt the muscles of my face quiver with the exact expression that should be there.

"Yes, sir," I replied, with the exact tone of eagerness I had practised so often. Gillette took up his lines. The scene was going well. The house hung breathless on every word.

"Don't look at the royal box," I repeated to myself, feeling

78

an almost irresistible longing to turn my head in that direction, and stiffening my neck against it.

I did not know who was in the box and would have been no wiser if I had looked, for I had never seen the royal family, but I learned later. The late King Edward himself was present, with Queen Alexandra, the King of Greece, Prince Christian[1] and the Duke of Connaught. Prince Christian, who was a personal friend of William Gillette, came often to see him act, but this was an unusually brilliant party.

I stood tense, waiting for my cue. It came at last.

"Billy, I want you to watch the thieves," said Sherlock Holmes.

It was a thrilling moment in the play. I must be silent just long enough—not too long—before I spoke. I heard my heart beat in the pause; the audience waited, tense. The house was silent.

Then, in the stillness, we heard a murmur from Prince Christian, and an impatient stage whisper in reply from the King of Greece.

"Don't tell me—don't tell me; I want to see it," he said. "Jove, watch that youngster!"

The tension of my nerves broke. William Gillette, in an effort to save the dramatic moment of the scene, repeated, "Billy, I want you to watch the thieves." And, while the house gazed at me, I turned my head and looked full at the royal box.

The audience was stunned. It sat dumb, in frozen horror. There was an awful silence, while I stood helpless, gazing at the King of Greece, and he stared back at me with slowly widening eyes. Then his face broke into little lines; they ran down from his eyes to his mouth; it widened into a smile. A sudden chuckle from King Edward[2] broke the terrible stillness. again we heard the voice of the King of Greece:

"By Jove! Ha! Ha!"

I tore my eyes away and continued the scene through a

79

haze. We finished it before a silent house. The curtain fell. Then, led by the royal box, a storm of applause arose. We took our curtain call—I was on the stage of a great West End theater, bowing before applauding crowds, in the company of one of the greatest actors in London. The voice of royalty itself had been heard speaking of my acting. I was dizzy with exultation.

The curtain fell for the last time and I strutted proudly from the stage, looking from one to another of the company, eager to meet their envious looks. They hurried to their dressing-rooms without a glance at me. No one spoke. There was a strained chill feeling in the atmosphere. I passed Mr. Postham and he hurried by me as if I was not there.

A feeling of trouble and loneliness grew upon me while I touched up my make-up for the second scene, though I told myself as confidently as possible that my looking at the royal box could not have been so bad, since the King of Greece had smiled and Mr. Postham had said nothing. Yet I would have been more at ease if he had sworn at me.

I threw myself into the work of the remaining scenes with all the skill I had learned, and I felt that I was doing them well, but the cold feeling of uncertainty and doubt grew upon me. At last the final curtain fell. Then for the first time that evening the eyes of the whole company turned on me. They lingered on the stage, waiting. Mr. Postham walked slowly out and looked at me quietly.

"Well, it went well, didn't it?" I said cockily to him, saying savagely to myself that I had been the hit of the evening. My words fell on a dead silence, while Mr. Postham continued to look at me, and little by little I felt myself growing very small and would have liked to go away, but could not.

"I suppose you realize what you did," Mr. Postham said, after a long time, and paused. I opened my mouth, but could not say a word.

"It is fortunate—very fortunate—that His Majesty—was pleased—to overlook it," Mr. Postham continued slowly. He paused again. "Fined three pounds," he said briskly, then, and walked away. So I went meekly from the scene of my first appearance in a good theater under the scornful and surprised glances of the other actors, who had expected to see that part taken from me, and I said bitterly to myself that if *this* was the reward of talent on the stage—!

I did good work that season with William Gillette, as all the press notices showed. Every morning, lying luxuriously in bed in my lodgings, I pored over the London journals, seizing eagerly on every comment on my acting, reading and rereading it. I was the "most promising young actor on the English stage," I was "doing clever work," I was "the best Billy London has seen yet." To me, as I gazed at these notices, William Gillette was merely "also mentioned." I felt that I alone was making the play a success and I walked afterward up and down the Strand in a glow of pride and self-confidence, dressed in all the splendor money could buy, swinging my cane, nodding carelessly to the men I knew and picturing them saying to each other after I had passed, "He is the great actor at the Duke of York's Theater. I knew him once."

The season was drawing to a close and, learning that William Gillette was returning to America, I confidently expected nothing less than an invitation to return with him, when one day I arrived at the theater early and found a note awaiting me. I tore it open carelessly and read:

"Will you please call at St. James' Theater to-morrow afternoon? I should like to see you.

"Mrs. Kendal."[3]

"Oh, ho! Mrs. Kendal!" I said to myself. "Well, she will have to offer something good to get *me!*"

In which I refuse an offer to play in the provinces; make my final appearance as Billy at the Duke of York's Theater; and suffer a bitter disappointment.

I assumed a slightly glanced through the Mrs. Kendal! The London. Well, I **18** bored air while I note again. Oh, yes, greatest actress in would call on her if she liked; I would just drop in and see what she had to offer. Something good, no doubt, but I should soon show her that it would have to be something very good indeed if she hoped to get *me*.

I flipped the note under the dressing-table and began to make up, wondering what America would prove to be like, picturing to myself the enthusiasm of American reporters when it was known that William Gillette was bringing England's greatest boy actor to New York with him.

"Curtain!" cried the call boy down the corridors. I called him in, hastily scribbled off a note to Mrs. Kendal, saying that I would call at twelve next day, and gave it to the call boy to post. Then I went out, nodding affably to the other actors, and took my place in the wings to await my cue.

"Too bad the season's closing, isn't it?" said Irene Vanbrugh,[1] who stood beside me.

"Oh, it's been a pleasant season enough, as seasons go," I replied carelessly. "The deuce of it is, there's no rest between 'em when one has made a hit. Rehearsals and all that."

"Y-yes," she said, looking at me queerly.

"And it's such a bore, so many people after one," I continued. "Now, there's Mrs. Kendal, very pleasant woman and all that—had another note from her just now. Suppose I'll have to run around and see her again."

"Oh, I say, Mrs. Kendal—not really!" Miss Vanbrugh cried, in such a tone of awe that it annoyed me. Mrs. Kendal was well enough, I said to myself, but I was the greatest boy actor in England. I took my cue confidently, glad not to be bothered with any more of Miss Vanbrugh's conversation.

The next day at noon I arrived at Mrs. Kendal's hotel, humming a bit and swinging a new cane, very well pleased with myself, for the notices in the London journals had been very good indeed that day. I noticed that the lift boy recognized me and seemed properly impressed, and I stepped into Mrs. Kendal's sitting-room disposed to be quite affable to her.

She was not there. I waited five minutes and still she had not come. I began to be irritated. What, keeping me waiting! I glanced at my watch, walked up and down a minute, very much bored with such lack of consideration on her part. Then I determined to leave and show her I was not to be trifled with in such a manner. Just as I took up my cane the door opened and Mrs. Kendal entered. She was a pleasant matronly-looking woman with tired lines around her eyes and a quiet gentle manner.

"I'm afraid I have just a minute," I said, ostentatiously looking at my watch again.

"I'm very sorry to have kept you waiting," she answered in a soft low voice. "We understand your season with Mr. Frohman is ending next week. Mr. Kendal and I have seen your work. We are taking out a company for a forty-weeks' tour in the provinces, and there is a part with us which we think you would fill very well."

I looked at her with raised eyebrows.

"In the provinces?" I said coldly. "I am very sorry, madam, but I could not think of leaving London." I took up my cane again and rose briskly.

Mrs. Kendal looked at me a moment with a tired smile

about her lips. Then she rose, said that in that case she regretted having taken up my time, and told me goodbye very pleasantly.

"She sees she can not offer *me* anything!" I said proudly to myself, putting back my shoulders importantly as I came down in the lift. I walked through the hotel lounging-room with a quick brisk step, called a cab and said to the driver in a loud voice, so the bystanders might guess who I was, "Duke of York's Theater, and be quick about it, my man!"

I awaited confidently an offer from Frohman to bring me to New York with William Gillette, determining when it came to insist on an increase in salary. Every evening I expected to find a note from him in my dressing-room, and I met the gloomy glances of the other actors with a wise smile and a knowing look. They might be troubled with the prospect of an uncertain future, I said to myself, but I was secure. I had made the hit of the piece, as the nightly applause showed.

The last week of *Sherlock Holmes* drew to a close, and with a sinking heart I realized that no offer had come from Frohman. I played my part every night with all the skill I knew, and hearing the house echo and echo again with loud applause, I said to myself, "*Now* Frohman will see how badly he needs me!" But still there was no word from him.

The last night came, and behind the scenes there was such a deep gloom that one could almost feel it like a fog. There was no joking in the dressing-rooms, the actors moodily made up and walked about the corridors afterward with strained anxious faces or laughed in a manner more gloomy than silence. The company was breaking up, no one knew what part he might find next, and all faced the prospect of wearily walking the Strand again, struggling to get a hearing with the agents, hoping against hope for a chance, growing shabbier and hungrier as they waited and hoped and saw the weeks going by.

For the last time I played Billy; for the last time I met Mr. Gillette's kindly glance and felt him pat my shoulder, saying, "Well done, Billy!" while the audience applauded. We stood together on the stage, bowing and smiling, while the curtain rose and fell and rose again and applause came over the footlights in crashing waves. Then the curtain fell for the last time.

"It's over," said Mr. Gillette, his shoulders drooping with weariness. Then he spoke a word or two of farewell to each of us and went to his dressing-room. The actors hurriedly took off their make-up and scattered, calling to one another in the corridor. "Well, so long, old man!" "See you later, Mabel, tata!" "Wait a minute, I'm coming!" "Good luck old fellow!"

I dressed slowly, unable to believe that this was the last night and that there was no offer from Mr. Frohman. Mr. Gillette was still in his dressing-room. I walked up and down outside his door debating whether or not to tap on it and ask him if there had not been a mistake.

"I was the hit of the play, wasn't I?" I said defiantly to myself, but a great wave of doubt and depression had come over me and I could not bring myself to knock on that door. Suddenly it opened and Mr. Gillette came out dressed for the street. Behind him I saw the Japanese servant carrying a bag.

"Mr. Gillette," I said boldly, though my knees were unsteady. "Aren't you taking any of the company to America with you?"

"Er—oh, it's you!" he said, startled, for he had almost stumbled against me in the gloom. "No; oh, no; I'm not taking any one with me. You were a very good Billy, Charles. I hope you get something good very soon. Goodbye."

**In which my fondest hopes
are shattered by cold reality; I learn
the part played by luck on the Strand;
and receive an unexpected appeal for help.**

19

I stood there watching Mr. Gillette's back receding down the corridor. I felt stunned, unable to realize that he was really going. I could not believe that it was all over, that he did not mean to take me to America after all. He stopped once and my heart gave a great leap and began to pound loudly, but he only spoke to some one he met and then went on. He turned a corner, the little Japanese servant turned the corner after him, carrying the bag. They were gone.

I went back into my dressing-room then and made a little bundle of my stage clothes and make-up box. The stage hands had finished clearing the stage; it was bare and dim when I crossed it and came out through the stage door for the last time. A cold gray fog was drifting down the deserted street and I wished to take a cab, but it came to me suddenly that I had no part now and could not afford it. I tucked my bundle under my arm and set out on foot for my lodgings.

All the way it seemed to me that I was in a bad dream—a dream where I must walk on and on mechanically through an unreal world of blurred lights and swirling grayness. I climbed the stairs to my lodgings at last, still with a dull hazy feeling of unreality, lighted the gas and sat down on my bed with the bundle beside me. Then it came upon me sharply that it was all true. The season was over. I was not going to America. I had only a few pounds and no prospect of getting another part.

I unfolded the little suit I had worn as Billy and looked at it for a long time, suffering as only a sensitive boy of fifteen can when he sees all his brightest hopes come to nothing. I walked

86

up and down, clenching my hands and wishing that I might die. It was almost dawn when I folded the little suit, put it away in the farthest corner of a closet and crawled miserably to bed.

Next morning I felt brighter. After all, I had made a big hit as Billy; there must be any number of managers in London who would be glad to get me. There were no letters for me in the mail, but I said to myself that I must give them time. I would put an advertisement in *The Strand*, mentioning that I was "resting," and they would come around all right. I wrote it out carefully, dressed my best and took it down to *The Strand* office myself so there would be no delay. Then I went to see my mother and told her lightly that I had not decided just what offer to accept. I could not trouble her, for she had not recovered her strength fully and could only lie on her couch and smile happily at me, proud of my great success.

All that month my hopes gradually faded while I went from agent to agent trying to get a part. At first my name got me an interview with the agent immediately, but each one I saw told me quite courteously, quite briskly, that he had nothing whatever to offer me and I came out of each office with a sinking heart, holding my haughty pose with difficulty.

I got up early every morning to see as many agents as possible during the day, and although before the other actors I still kept my pose of being a great success, merely dropping in to pass the time of day with the agent, I felt panic growing within me. My small stock of money was gone. I pawned my watch, my clothes, at last even my bag, and hoarded the pennies desperately, dining in small, dirty eating houses on two-pence worth of stew.

I still bravely made a show of importance and success when I met the other actors tramping the Strand, lying miserably to them as they lied to me while we spent hours in the outer offices of the agents, bullied by the office boy, waiting hopelessly for a chance to see the agents. The season was far advanced and chances for a part grew smaller daily, but it was incredible to me that I should not find something—I who had made such a hit with William Gillette! Every morning I started out saying to myself that surely I should get something that day, and every night I crawled wearily into my lodgings, tired and discouraged, avoiding the landlady.

One day I determined to stand it no longer. I carefully trimmed my frayed collar and the cuffs, brushed my suit and hat and went to the offices of the biggest agent of all, Mr. Braithewaite. He was a courteous gentleman and had always welcomed me politely. I walked in with my most important air.

"Mr. Braithewaite, I must have a part," I said briskly. "You know my work. You know I made a big hit with William Gillette. Now, I'll take anything you can give me, I don't care how small it is or what it pays. Haven't you something in a provincial company—even a walking-on part?"

He thought it over for some time in silence, while I heard my heart beating. Then he said slowly, "Well, there is a part—I will see. You come in to-morrow."

I came out whistling merrily, stepping high with a dizzy feeling that the pavement was unsteady under my feet. I was sure by his manner that he meant to have a part for me and all my self-complacency was restored. I flipped my cane as I passed the doors of the other agents, saying to myself, "Oh, ho! You'll see what you have missed!" and thinking that I would carelessly drop in and tell those who had treated me worst how well I was doing as soon as I should have the part. That night I spent one of my last two shillings for dinner, feasting on tripe and onions and ale in great spirits.

Next day, nervous with hope, I hurried to Mr. Braithewaite's offices and walked in confidently, so wrapped in my own thoughts that I did not notice that no actors were waiting as usual. I said briskly to the office boy, trying to keep my voice natural and steady, "Tell Mr. Braithewaite I am here. I have an appointment."

He looked at me with a long shrill whistle of surprise. Then, with great enjoyment in telling startling news, he said, "Don't tell me you 'aven't 'eard! 'E was shot by burglars last night. 'E's 'anging between life and death right now."

I remembered I stumbled on the stairs once or twice, feeling numb all over and not able to walk steady. The bright sunlight outside seemed to jeer at me. My last hope was gone. I could not muster courage to start again on the endless tramp up and down the Strand or to face the other actors. I went back to my lodgings. The landlady met me on the stairs and looked steadily at me with tight lips and an eye which said, "I know you have only a shilling; what are you going to do about the rent?" I went hurriedly past her and climbed up to my room bitterly humiliated.

There was a letter waiting for me on the mantel. I seized it and tore it open, wild thoughts that at last I had an offer whirling in my brain. It was dated Paris. I looked at the signature— Sydney! Good old Sydney, I said to myself; he will help me. Then I read the letter.

"Dear Charlie," it said. "Your press notices are received and no one is gladder than I am. You know we always knew you would be a great success. How does it feel to have all London applauding? I wager you enjoy cutting a dash[2] on the Strand, what? Well, Charlie, I am in the profession now, and not so great a success as you yet, but I have a prospect of a part in a couple of weeks perhaps. You know how it goes. Can you lend me five pounds, or even three, till I get a part? Love to mother and congratulations again to the clever one of the family.

"Your brother, Sydney."

**In which I try to
drown my troubles in
liquor and find them worse than
before; try to make a living by hard
work and meet small success; and find myself
at last in a hospital bed, saying a surprising thing.**

I stared stupidly at **20** Sydney's letter for a minute and then I re- read it slowly. It seemed like a horrible mockery — "cutting a dash on the Strand" — "The clever one of the family." And he wanted to borrow five pounds—or three—when I had only a shilling the world.

It was the most bitter humiliation of my life. I who had always been so sure of my talent, who had patronized Sydney and promised so grandly to help him if he ever needed it and sent him the press notices of my great success with a condescending little note saying that it made no difference to me, I remembered him as fondly as ever—I could not send him a penny, or even buy food for myself.

After a while I took out a sheet of paper and tried to write to him, but I could not manage it. I made several beginnings and chewed my pen a long time, while my shame and misery grew until I could bear it no longer. I put on my hat and went out.

Then, having made so many mistakes already and lost so much by them that I could not endure my own thoughts, I tried to make matters better by making them worse. A little way down the street was a barroom. Its windows were brightly lighted, casting a warm shining glow out into the foggy twilight, and I could hear men laughing inside. I went in, threw my shilling on the bar and called for whisky. It was strong raw stuff and made my throat burn, but standing there by the bar I felt a little self-esteem come back and said to myself that I was not beaten yet. I pushed the change back to the bartender and asked for another glass of the same.

I remember telling some one loudly who I was and declaring that I was the greatest actor in London. Somebody paid for more drinks and I drank again and told very witty stories and became amazingly clever and successful, laughing loudly and boasting of my dancing. I did dance, and there was great applause, and more drinks and a great deal of noise, and I became fast friends with some one whom I promised to give a fine part in my next play and we drank again. In a word, I got gloriously drunk.

I woke up sometime the next day in an alley, feeling very ill and more discouraged and depressed than before. When I slowly realized what had happened and that I had not a cent in the world, nor anything else but the rumpled, dirty clothes I wore, I sat with my head in my hands and groaned and loathed the thought of living. I did not want ever to stir again, but after a while I got up dizzily and managed to come out into the street. I knew I must do something.

I was in the North End of London.[1] The dingy warehouses and dirty cobbled streets, through which the heavy vans rumbled, drawn by big, clumsy-footed horses, reminded me of the days in Covent Garden market, and I thought of the way I had lived there and wondered if I could find something to do there now. The thought of the Strand, where I had walked so many weeks, was hideous to me. I hated it. I said to myself then that I would never be an actor again.

I found a watering trough and washed in it, splashing the cold water over my head until I felt refreshed. I determined not to go back to my lodgings, the few things I had left there would settle the small score and I did not want to face the landlady. The thought of my mother was more than I could face, too, but I said to myself that Mrs. Dobbs would keep her until I could get some work and send her the rent. Then I set out to hunt for a job.

I found one that afternoon. It was hard work, rolling

heavy casks from one end of a warehouse to the other and helping to load them on vans. I was about fifteen at the time and slight, but some way I managed to do the work, though aching in every muscle long before the day was over. I got ten shillings a week and permission to sleep in the vans in the court behind the warehouse. I held the place almost a week before the foreman lost patience with me and found some one else to take my place.

I had made friends with several of the men, and one of them got me a place as driver for a milk company. This was easier work, though I had to be at it soon after midnight, driving through the cold dark morning, the horses almost pulling my arms from the sockets with every toss of their heavy heads, and delivering the milk in dark area-ways, where I stumbled sleepily on the steps. I had money enough now to pay for lodging in a dirty room without a window in a cheap lodging house, and I breakfasted and lunched on buns and stolen milk. I could not bring myself to visit my mother, but I sent her a few shillings in a letter and wrote that I was well and busy, so that she need not worry.

Then one morning the loss of the stolen milk was discovered. I had been unusually hungry and drunk too much of it. The boss swore at me furiously, and again I was out of a job. I was wandering up the street wondering what I could do next when I saw a great crowd about the door of a glass factory. It was still early, about four o'clock in the morning, but hundreds of men and boys were massed there waiting. I pushed my way into the crowd and asked what had happened.

Most of the boys looked at me sullenly and would not answer, but one of them showed me an advertisement. It read: "Boy wanted to work in glass factory. Seven shillings a week." My heart gave a leap, I might be the lucky one! I pushed as close to the door as I could and waited. At seven o'clock the door opened and the crowd began to sway in excitement, each one crying out eager words to the man in the doorway.

I climbed nimbly up the back of the man before me, and gripping his neck with my knees, called vigorously, "Here I am, sir!" My theatrical training had taught me how to use my voice, the man heard me above the uproar and looked at me.

"I want an experienced boy in the cooling room," he said. "Had any experience?"

"Oh, yes, sir!" I answered, while the man on whose back I crouched tried to pull me down.

"All right, come in and I'll try you," the man in the doorway answered, and while the others fell back, disappointed, I crushed through the crowd and rushed in.

The work proved to be carrying bottles from the furnace room to the cooling place. I went at it with a will, hurrying from the terrifically heated room into the cold air with the heavy trays and back again as fast as I could. No matter how fast I ran there were always more bottles waiting than I could get out in time and the half-naked men, sweltering in the furnace heat, swore at me while I jumped back and forth. At noon, too exhausted to eat, I lay down in a corner to rest, but before my aching muscles had stopped throbbing the afternoon work began and the foreman was calling to me to hurry.

My head ached with a queer jumping pain and I was so dizzy that I dropped a tray of bottles and blundered into the edge of the door more than once, but I shut my teeth tight and kept on. I did not mean to lose that job. It meant nearly two dollars a week.

I kept at it till late that afternoon, dripping with perspiration while my teeth chattered and my legs grew more unsteady with every trip. Then, as I bent before a furnace to pick up a tray there was a sudden glare of light and heat, a tremendous, crashing explosion. Everything swirled into flame and then into darkness.

When I came to myself again I was in an infirmary bed, just a mass of burning pain wrapped in bandages, and I heard myself saying vigorously, while some tried to quiet me, "I am the greatest actor in London. I tell you I am the greatest actor in London."

In which I encounter the inexorable rules of a London hospital, causing much consternation; fight a battle with pride; and unexpectedly enter an upsetting situation.

I did not find the **21** hospital unpleasant, for I had enough to eat there, and although my burns were painful, it was a delight to be in a clean bed. I lay there three weeks, quite contented, and all day long, and when I could not sleep at night, I thought over my stage experience and the mistakes I had made in it and finally grew able to laugh at myself. It is the only valuable thing I have ever learned.

Life trips people up and makes them fall on their noses at every step. It takes the very qualities that make success and turns them into stumbling blocks, and when we go tumbling over them the only thing to do is to get up and laugh at ourselves. If I had not been a precocious, self-satisfied, egotistic boy, able to imagine unreal things and think them true, I could never have been a success on the stage, and if I had been none of those things I would not have thrown away the opportunity Mrs. Kendal gave me and been a failure. That is an Irish bull,[1] but life must have its little joke, and there you are.

At the end of the three weeks my burns were sufficiently healed, and one day the nurse came and told me that I could leave the hospital.

"Very well," I said, "but how? I have no clothes."

"My goodness!" she said. "I—but you can't stay here, you know."

"Will you lend me a sheet?" I asked. "I must wear something."

"On, no; we couldn't do that," she replied, and went away, dazed by the problem. I lay there grinning to myself and ate my supper with good appetite. The next day the doctor came and looked at me and scratched his head and said testily that I was well enough to go and must go; I must get some clothes.

"How can I get clothes unless I go and earn them, and how can I earn them if I don't have any?" I asked him.

"Isn't there any way to get this lad any clothes?" he said to the nurse. She said she did not know, there had never been a case just like it before. She would ask the superintendent. She came back with the superintendent, and all three of them looked at me. The superintendent said firmly that I must go, that it was against the rules for me to stay any longer. I replied firmly that I would not go into the streets of London without any clothes. The superintendent shut her lips firmly and went away.

There was a great sensation in the hospital. My own garments had been destroyed in the explosion. The rules demanded that I go, but the rules provided no clothes for me; I would not go without clothes, and no one could feel my position unreasonable. The hospital swayed under the strain of the situation.

The next afternoon a representative of the Society for the Relief of the Deserving Poor called to see me. She asked a dozen questions, wrote the answers in a book and went away. Another day passed. The nurses were pale with suspense. No clothes arrived.

Wild rumors circulated that I was to be wrapped in a blanket and sent out in the night, but they were contradicted by the fact that the rules did not provide for the loan of the blanket. Friendly patients urged me to be firm, kindly nurses told me not to worry, the superintendent was reported baffled by the rules of the charitable organizations, which did not provide for clothing patients in the charity hospitals.

Some natural resentment was felt against me for not fitting

any rules, but the food came regularly and I ate and slept comfortably. On the fourth day, when it was felt that something desperate must be done, the situation suddenly cleared. Sydney arrived.

The representative of the S. R. D. P. had called at my mother's address in the course of her investigations as to my worthiness and found him there. He was playing in an East End theater and very much worried about my disappearance. On hearing of my plight he had hastened to the rescue and cut short my life of ease and plenty under the unwilling shelter of the hospital rules. He brought me clothes, and I departed, to the disappointment of the other patients who felt it an anticlimax.

Well fed and rested, and with the stimulus of Sydney's encouragement, I started again my search for a part. Much as I had hated the Strand at times, it was like coming home again to be tramping up and down the agents' stairs and exchanging boasts with the other actors while I waited in the outer offices. Usually I waited long hours, only to be sent away at last with the office boy's curt announcement that the agent would see no one, and when sometimes I did penetrate into the inner offices I met always the same, "Nothing in sight. Things are very quiet just now. Drop in again." Then I came out, with my old jaunty air hiding my bitter disappointment and tramped down the stairs and along the Strand and up to another office, to wait again.

Mrs. Dobbs, my mother's landlady, moved to Sweetbay, and being fond of my mother and her sweet gentle ways, had consented to take her there for a moderate rate. Sydney and I lived together in a bed-sitting-room in Alfred Place on very scant fare and I hated to face him at night.

"Well, any news?" he always asked, pleasantly enough, but I dreaded the moment and having to say, "No, not yet." It hurt my pride terribly, and after several months of it the misery of that first moment of meeting Sydney drove me into hurting my pride even more in another way.

"Look here, what's all this talk about playing lead and being with William Gillette worth to you?" an agent said to me one day. "You'll take anything you can jolly well get, no matter what it is, won't you? Well, Dailey, over at the Grand, is putting out a comedy next week with *Casey's Circus*.[2] There's fifteen parts, none of 'em cast yet. Go and see what you can do."

I came out of his office in an agony of indecision for while it was true that I had said to myself many times that I would take any part I could get, I had never imagined myself acting in *Casey's Circus*. All the pride that had survived those months of discouragement writhed at the idea—I who had been a hit in a West End theater acting a low vulgar comedy in dirty fourth-rate houses—why, it was not so good a chance as my part in *Rags to Riches!* I said savagely that I would not do it. Then I thought of Sydney and bit my lips and hesitated.

In the end, burning with shame and resentment, I went to see Dailey. At least a hundred third-rate actors packed the stairs to his office and more were blocking the street and sitting on the curbs before his door opened. I was crushed in the crowd of them, smothered by rank perfume and the close thick air of the dirty stairs, and I hated myself and the situation more every minute of the three hours I waited there, but I stayed, half hoping he would not give me a part. At least I could feel then that I had done all I could.

At last my turn came. I straightened my hat, squared my shoulders and marched in, determined to be very haughty and dignified. Mr. Dailey, a fat red-faced man, with his waistcoat unbuttoned, sat by a desk chewing a big cigar.

"Mr. Dailey," I said, "I——" I don't know how it happened. My foot slipped. I tried to straighten up, slipped again, fell on all fours over a chair, which fell over on me, and sat up on the floor with the chair in my lap. "——want a part," I finished, furious.

Mr. Dailey howled and laughed and choked, and held his sides and laughed again and choked, purple in the face.

"You'll do," he said at last. "Great entrance! Great! Ten shillings a week and railway fares; what do you say to that, my lad?"

"I won't take it," I retorted.

In which I attempt to
be serious and am funny instead;
seize the opportunity to get a raise in
pay; and again consider coming to America.

Mr. Dailey would not  let me go, but, still wiping tears of laughter from his eyes, began shilling by shilling to raise his offer. My entirely unintentional comedy entrance had pleased him mightily, and indeed, as soon as I saw he took it as a deliberate effort on my part, I began to be not a little proud of it myself. It was not every one, I said to myself, who could fall over a chair so comically as that!

Cheered and emboldened by this reflection, I drove a shrewd bargain, and at last, persuaded by the offer of a pound a week and a long engagement if I could keep on being funny, I consented to become a member of *Casey's Circus*, and returned whistling to our lodgings, able to face Sydney with some degree of pride because I had an engagement at last.

We began rehearsals next day in a very dirty dark room over a public house—fifteen ragged, hungry-looking, sallow-faced boys desperately being funny under the direction of a fat greasy-looking manager who smelled strongly of ale. It was difficult work for me at first. Being funny is at best a hard job, and being funny in those conditions, which I heartily detested, seemed at first almost impossible. More than once, when the manager swore at me more than usual, I felt like throwing the whole thing up and would have done so but for the dread of going back to the endless tramping up and down the Strand and being a burden on Sydney.

Casey's Circus was putting on that season a burlesque of persons in the public eye, and I was cast for the part of Doctor Body,[1] a patent-medicine faker, who was drawing big crowds

100

on the London street corners and selling a specific for all the ills of man and beast at a shilling the bottle. Watching him one afternoon, I was seized with a great idea. I would let the manager rehearse me all he jolly well liked, but when the opening night came I would play Doctor Body as he really was—I would put on such a marvelous character delineation that even the lowest music-hall audience would recognize it as great acting and I would be rescued by some good manager and brought back to a West End theater.

The idea grew upon me. Despising with all my heart the cheap, clap-trap burlesque which the manager tried to drill into me, I paid only enough attention to it to get through rehearsals somehow, hurrying out afterward to watch Doctor Body and to practise before the mirror in our lodgings my own idea of the part. I felt that I did it well and thrilled with pride at the thought of playing it soon with the eye of a great manager upon me.

The night of the opening came and I hurried to the dirty makeshift dressing-room in a cheap East End music-hall with all the sensations of a boy committing his first burglary. I must manage to make up as the real Doctor Body and to get on the stage before I was caught. Once on the stage, without the burlesque make-up which I was supposed to wear, I knew I could make the part go. I painted my face stealthily among the uproar and quarrels of the other fourteen boys, who were all in the same dressing-room fighting over the mirrors and hurling epithets and make-up boxes at one another.

The air tingled with excitement. The distracted manager, thrusting his head in at the door, cried with oaths that Casey himself was in front and he'd stand for no nonsense. We could hear him rushing away, swearing at the scene shifters, who had made some error in placing the set. The audience was in bad humor; we could faintly hear it hooting and whistling. It had thrown rotten fruit at the act preceding ours. In the confusion I managed to make up and to get into my clothes, troubled by the size of the high hat I was to wear, which came down over my ears. I stuffed it with paper to keep it at the proper angle on my head, and trembling with nervousness, but sure of myself when I should get on the stage, I stole out of the dressing-room and stationed myself in the darkest part of the wings.

The boy who appeared first was having a bad time of it, missing his cues and being hissed and hooted by the audience. The manager rushed up to me, caught sight of my make-up and stopped aghast.

"'Ere, you can't go on like that!" he said in a furious whisper, catching my arm.

"Let me alone; I know what I'm doing!" I cried angrily, wrenching myself from him. My great plan was not to be spoiled now at the last minute. The manager reached for me again, purple with wrath, but, quick as an eel, I ducked under his arm, seized the cane I was to carry and rushed on to the stage half a minute too soon.

Once in the glare of the footlights I dropped into the part, determined to play it, play it well, and hold the audience. The other boy, whose part I had spoiled, confused by my unexpected appearance, stammered in his lines and fell back. I advanced slowly, impressively, feeling the gaze of the crowd, and, with a carefully studied gesture, hung my cane—I held it by the wrong end! Instead of hanging on my arm, as I expected, it clattered on the stage. Startled, I stooped to pick it up, and my high silk hat fell from my head. I grasped it, put it on quickly, and, paper wadding falling out, I found my whole head buried in its black depths.

A great burst of laughter came from the audience. When, pushing the hat back, I went desperately on with my serious lines, the crowd roared, held its sides, shrieked with mirth till it gasped. The more serious I was, the funnier it struck the audience. I came off at last, pursued by howls of laughter and wild applause, which called me back again. I had made the hit of the evening.

"That was a good bit of business, my lad," Mr. Casey himself said, coming behind the scenes and meeting me in the wings when finally the audience let me leave the stage the second time. "Your idea?"

"Oh, certainly," I replied airily. "Not bad, I flatter myself— er—but of course not what I might do at that." And, seizing the auspicious moment, I demanded a raise to two pounds a week and got it.

The next week I was headlined as "Charles Chaplin, the funniest actor in London," and *Casey's Circus* packed the house wherever it was played. I had stumbled on the secret of being funny—unexpectedly. An idea, going in one direction, meets an opposite idea suddenly. "Ha! Ha!" you shriek. It works every time.

I walk on to the stage, serious, dignified, solemn, pause before an easy chair, spread my coat-tails with an elegant gesture—and sit on the cat. Nothing funny about it, really, especially if you consider the feelings of the cat. But you laugh. You laugh because it is unexpected. Those little nervous shocks make you laugh; you can't help it. Peeling onions makes you weep, and seeing a fat man carrying a custard pie slip and sit down on it makes you laugh.

In the two years I was with *Casey's Circus* I gradually gave up my idea of playing great parts on the dramatic stage. I grew to like the comedy work, to enjoy hearing the bursts of laughter from the audience, and getting the crowd in good humor and keeping it so was a nightly frolic for me. Then, too, by degrees all my old self-confidence and pride came back, with the difference, indeed, that I did not take them too seriously, as before, but merely felt them like a pleasant inner warmth as I walked on the Strand and saw the envious looks of other actors not so fortunate.

One day, walking there in this glow of success, swinging my cane with a nonchalant air and humming to myself, I met the old comedian who had been with the *Rags to Riches* company.

"I say, old top," he said eagerly, falling into step with me, "do a chap a favor, won't you now? There's a big chance with Karno[2]—I have it on the quiet he's planning to take a company to America, and half a dozen parts not cast. Good pickings, what? I can't get a word with the beggar, but he'd listen to you. See what you can do for yourself and then say a good word for me, won't you, what?"

**In which I startle
a promoter; dream a great
triumph in the land of skyscrapers
and buffalo; and wait long for a message.**

America! Fred **23** Karno!
The words went off like rockets in my
mind, bursting into thousands of sparkling ideas. Fred Karno, the biggest
comedy producer in London—a man who could by a word
make me the best-known comedian in Europe! I could already
see the press notices—"Charlie Chaplin, the great comedian, in
the spectacular Karno production—." And America, that
strange country across the sea, where I had heard men thought
no more of half-crowns than we thought of six-pences; New
York, where the buildings were ten, twenty, even thirty floors
high, and the sky blazed with enormous signs in electric light;
Chicago, where the tinned meat came from, and, between vast
plains covered with buffalo and wild forests, where, as the train
plunged through them at tremendous speed, I might see from
the compartment window the American red men around their
camp-fires! The man at my side was saying that there was a
chance to go to America with Karno.

"Go see him, old chap; please do," the old comedian
begged me. "He'll see you, quick enough, though he keeps me
waiting in his offices like a dog. And say a good word for me;
just get me a chance to see him. I've put you on to a good
thing, what? You won't forget old friends, will you now?"

"Er—certainly not, certainly not!" I assured him loftily.
"Now I think of it, Freddie was mentioning to me the other day
something about sending a company to America. Next time I
see him—the very next time, on my word—I'll mention your
name. You can depend on it."

Then, waving away his fervid thanks and declining kindly his suggestion to have a glass of bitter, I hailed a cab and drove away, eager to be alone and think over the dazzling prospect. My own small success seemed flat enough beside it. America—Fred Karno! After all, why not? I asked myself. I could make people laugh; Karno did not have a man who could do it better. Just let me have a chance to show him what I could do!

So excited that I could feel the blood beating in my temples and every nerve quivering, I beat on the cab window with my cane and called to the driver to take me to Karno's offices quick. "An extra shilling if you do it in five minutes!" I cried, and sat on the edge of the seat as the cab lurched and swayed, hoping only that I could get there before all the parts were gone.

I walked into Karno's offices with a quick assured step, hiding my excitement under an air of haughty importance, though only a great effort kept my hand from trembling as I gave my card to the office boy. I swallowed hard and called to mind all the press notices I had received in the two years with *Casey's Circus* while I waited, trying to gain an assurance I did not feel, for Karno was a very big man, indeed. When the office boy returned and ushered me into the inner office I felt my knees unsteady under me.

"Ah, you got here quickly," Mr. Karno said pleasantly, waving me to a chair, and this unexpected reception completed my confusion.

"Oh, yes. I was—I happened to be going by," I replied, dazed.

Mr. Karno leaned back in his chair, carefully fitting his finger tips together and looked at me keenly with his lips pursed up. I said nothing more, being doubtful just what to say, and after a minute he sat up very briskly and spoke.

"As I mentioned in my note," he began, and the office

106

seemed to explode into fireworks about me. He had sent me a note. He wanted me, then. I could make my own terms. "And perhaps I could use you for next season," he finished whatever he had said.

"Yes," I said promptly. "In your American company."

"My American company? Well, no. That is still very indefinite," he replied. "But I can give you a good part with *Repairs* in the provinces. Thirty weeks, at three pounds."

"No, I would not consider that," I answered firmly. "I will take a part in your American company at six pounds." *Six* pounds—it was an enormous salary; twice as much as I had ever received. I was aghast as I heard the words, but I said doggedly to myself that I would stand by them. I was a great comedian; Fred Karno himself has sent for me; I was worth six pounds.

"*Six* pounds! It's unheard of. I never pay it," Mr. Karno said sharply.

"Six pounds, not a farthing less," I insisted.

"In that case I am afraid I can't use you. Good morning," he answered.

"Good morning," I said, and rising promptly I left the office.

That night I played as I had never played before. The audience howled with laughter from my entrance till my last exit and recalled me again and again, until I would only bow and back off. I carried in a pocket of my stage clothes the note from Mr. Karno, which I had found waiting at the theater, and I winked at myself triumphantly in the mirror while I took off my make-up.

"He'll come around. Watch me!" I said confidently, and not even Sydney's misgivings nor his repeated urgings to seize the chance with Karno at any salary could shake my determination.

"I'm going to America," I said firmly. "And I won't go

under six pounds. Living costs terrifically over there; all the lodgings have built-in baths and they charge double for it. I stand by six pounds and I'll get it, never fear."

In my own heart I had misgivings more than once in the months that followed without another message from Karno, but I set my teeth and vowed that, since I had said six pounds, six pounds it should be. And I worked at comedy effects all day long in our lodgings, falling over chairs and tripping over my cane for hours together, till I was black and blue, but prepared, when the curtain went up at night, to make the audience hold their sides and shriek helplessly with tears of laughter on their cheeks.

"Any news?" Sydney began to ask again every evening, but I managed always to say, "Not yet!" with cocky assurance. "He'll send for me, never fear," I said, warmed with the thought of the applause I was getting and the press notices.

The season with *Casey's Circus* was ending and I took care not to let any hint of my intention to leave reach the ears of the manager, but I refused to believe that I would be obliged to fall back on him. I looked eagerly every day for another note from Karno.

"Don't worry, I'll see you get your bit when the time is ripe," I told the old comedian whenever he importuned me for news, as he did frequently. "You know how it is, old top—you have to manage these big men just right."

At last the note came. It reached me at my lodgings early one morning, having been sent on from the theater, and I trembled with excitement while I dressed. I forced myself to eat breakfast slowly and to idle about a bit before starting for Karno's offices, not to reach them too early and appear too eager, but when at last I set out the cab seemed to do no more than crawl.

"Well, I find I can use you in the American company," Mr. Karno said.

"Very well," I replied nonchalantly.

"And—er—as to salary—," he began, but I cut in.

"Salary?" I said, shrugging my shoulders. "Why mention it? We went over that before," and I waved my hand carelessly. "Six pounds," I said airily.

He looked at me a minute, frowning. Then he laughed.

"All right, confound you!" he said, smiling, and took out the contract.

Three weeks later, booked for a solid year in the United States, looking forward to playing on the Keith circuit among the Eastern skyscrapers and on the Orpheum circuit[1] in the Wild West among the American red men, I stood on the deck of a steamer and saw the rugged sky-line of New York rising from the sea.

**In which I discover many
strange things in that strange
land, America; visit San Francisco
for the first time; and meet an astounding
reception in the offices of a cinematograph company.**

Now, since I was **24** twenty at the time,
four years ago, when I stood on the deck
of the steamer and saw America rising
into view on the horizon, it may seem
strange to some persons that I had no truer idea of this country
than to suppose just west of New York a wild country inhabited
by American Indians and traversed by great herds of buffalo.
It is natural enough, however, when one reflects that I had
spent nearly all my life in London, which is, like all great cities,
a most narrow-minded and provincial place, and that my only
schooling had been the little my mother was able to give me,
combined later with much eager reading of romances. Feni-
more Cooper, your own American writer, had pictured for me
this country as it was a hundred years ago, and what English
boy would suppose a whole continent could be made over in a
short hundred years?

So, while the steamer docked, I stood quivering with eagerness to be off into the wonders of that forest of skyscrapers
which is New York, with all the sensations of a boy transported
to Mars, or any other unknown world, where anything might
happen. Indeed, one of the strangest things—to my way of
thinking—which I encountered in the New World, was
brought to my attention a moment after I landed. At the very
foot of the gangplank Mr. Reeves, the manager of the American company,[1] who was with me, was halted by a very fat little
man, richly dressed, who rushed up and grasped him enthusiastically by both hands.

"Velgome! Velgome to our gountry!" he cried. "How are you, Reeves? How goes it?"

Mr. Reeves replied in a friendly manner, and the little man turned to me inquiringly. "Who's the kid?" he asked.

"This is Mr. Chaplin, our leading comedian," Mr. Reeves said, while I bristled at the word "kid." The fat man, I found, was Marcus Lowe, a New York theatrical producer.[2] He shook hands with me warmly and asked immediately, "Vell, and vot do you think of our gountry, young man?"

"I have never been in Berlin," I said stiffly. "I have never cared to go there," I added rudely, resenting his second reference to my youth.

"I mean America. How do you like America? This is our gountry now. We're all Americans together over here!" Marcus Loew said with real enthusiasm in his voice, and I drew myself up in haughty surprise. "My word, this *is* a strange country," I said to myself. Foreigners, and all that, calling themselves citizens! This is going rather far, even for a republic, even for America, where anything might happen.

That was the thing which most impressed me for weeks. Germans, it seemed, and English and Irish and French and Italians and Poles, all mixed up together, all one nation—it seemed incredible to me, like something against all the laws of nature. I went about in a continual wonder at it. Not even the high buildings, higher even than I had imagined, nor the enormous, flaming electric signs on Broadway, not the high, hysterical, shrill sound of the street traffic, so different from the heavy roar of London, was so strange to me as this mixing of races. Indeed, it was months before I could become accustomed to it, and months more before I saw how good it is, and felt glad to be part of such a nation myself.

We were playing a sketch called *A Night in a London Music-*

Hall,[3] which probably many people still remember. I was cast for the part of a drunken man, who furnished most of the comedy, and the sketch proved to be a great success, so that I played that one part continuously for over two years, traveling from coast to coast with it twice.

The number of American cities seemed endless to me, like the little bores the Chinese make, one inside the other, so that it seems no matter how many you take out, there are still more inside. I had imagined this country a broad wild continent, dotted sparsely with great cities—New York, Chicago, San Francisco—with wide distances between. The distances were there, as I expected, but there seemed no end to the cities. New York, Buffalo, Pittsburgh, Cincinnati, Columbus, Indianapolis, Chicago, St. Louis, Kansas City, Omaha, Denver—and San Francisco not even in sight yet! No Indians, either.

Toward the end of the summer we reached San Francisco the first time, very late, because the train had lost time over the mountains, so that there was barely time for us to reach the Orpheum and make up in time for the first performance. My stage hat was missing, there was a wild search for it, while we held the curtain and the house grew a little impatient, but we could not find it anywhere. At last I seized a high silk hat from the outraged head of a man who had come behind the scenes to see Reeves and rushed on to the stage. The hat was too loose. Every time I tried to speak a line it fell off, and the audience went into ecstasies. It was one of the best hits of the season, that hat.

It slid back down my neck, and the audience laughed; it fell over my nose, and they howled; I picked it up on the end of my cane, looked at it stupidly and tried to put the cane on my head, and they roared. I do not know the feelings of its owner, who for a time stood glaring at me from the wings, for when at last, after the third curtain call, I came off holding the much dilapidated hat in my hands, he had gone. Bareheaded, I suppose, and probably still very angry.

After the show I came out on the street into a cold gray fog, which blurred the lights and muffled the sound of my steps on the damp pavement, and, drawing great breaths of it into my lungs, I was happy. "For the lova Mike!" I said to Reeves, being very proud of my American slang. "This is a little bit of all right, what? Just like home, don't you know! What do you know about that!" And I felt that, next to London, I liked San Francisco, and was sorry we were to stay only two weeks.

We returned to New York, playing return dates on the "big time" circuits, and I almost regretted the close of the season and the return to London. The night we closed at Keith's I found a message waiting for me at the theater.

"We want you in the pictures. Come and see me and talk it over. Mack Sennett."[4]

"Who's Mack Sennett?" I asked Reeves, and he told me he was with the Keystone motion-picture company. "Oh, the cinematographs!" I said, for I knew them in London, and regarded them as even lower that the music-halls. I tore up the note and threw it away.

"I suppose we're going home next week?" I asked Reeves, and he said he thought not; the "little big time" circuits wanted us and he was waiting for a cable from Karno.

Early next day I called at his apartments, eager to learn what he had heard, for I wanted very much to stay in America another year, and saw no way to do it if Karno recalled the company. I did not think again of the note from Sennett, for I did not regard seriously an offer to go into the cinematographs. I was delighted to hear that we were going to stay, and left New York in great spirits, with the prospect of another year with *A Night in a London Music-Hall* in America.

Twelve months later, back in New York again, I received

another message from Mr. Sennett, to which I paid no more attention than to the first one. We were sailing for London the following month. One day, while I was walking down Broadway with a chance acquaintance, we passed the Keystone offices and my companion asked me to come in with him. He had some business with a man there. I went in, and was waiting in the outer office when Mr. Sennett came through and recognized me.

"Good morning, Mr. Chaplin, glad to see you! Come right in," he said cordially, and, ashamed to tell him I had not come in reply to his message, that indeed I had not meant to answer it at all, I followed him into his private office. I talked vaguely, waiting for an opportunity to get away without appearing rude. At last I saw it.

"Let's not beat about the bush any longer," Mr. Sennett said. "What salary will you take to come with the Keystone?" This was my chance to end the interview, and I grasped it eagerly.

"Two hundred dollars a week," I said, naming the most extravagant price which came into my head.

"All right," he replied promptly. "When can you start?"[5]

In which I find
that the incredible
has happened; burn my bridges
behind me and penetrate for the first time the
mysterious regions behind the moving-picture film.

"But—I said two week," I repeated Mr. Sennett's un- Two hundred dol- **25** hundred dollars a feebly, stunned by expected response. lars a week—forty pounds—he couldn't mean it! It was absolutely impossible.

"Yes. That's right. Two hundred dollars a week," Mr. Sennett said crisply. "When can you begin work?"

"Why—you know, I must have a two-year's contract at that salary," I said, feeling my way carefully, for I still could not credit this as a genuine offer.

"All right, we'll fix it up. Two years, two hundred—" he made a little memorandum on a desk pad, and something in the matter-of-fact way he did it convinced me that this incredible thing had actually happened. "Contract will be ready this afternoon, say at four o'clock. That will suit you? And we'd like you to start for California as soon as possible."

"Certainly. Oh, of course," I said, though still more confounded by this, for I did not see the connection between California and the cinematograph. More than anything else, however, I felt that I needed air and an opportunity to consider where I stood anyway, and what I was going to do.

I walked down Broadway in a daze. An actor for a cinematographic company—my mind shied at the thought. How were the confounded things made, anyhow? Still, two hundred dollars a week—what would happen if I could not do the work? I tried to imagine what it would be like. Acting before a machine—how could I tell whether I was funny or not? The machine would not laugh. Then suddenly I stopped short in a tangle of cross-street traffic and cried aloud, "Look here, you

115

could have got twice the money!" But instantly that thought was swept away again by my speculations about the work and my concern as to whether or not I could do it.

At four o'clock I returned to the Keystone offices, in a mood between exultation and panic, and signed the contract, beginning with a feeble scratch of the pen, but ending in a bold black scrawl. It was done; I was a moving-picture actor, and heaven only knew what would happen next!

"Can you start for California to-night?" Mr. Sennett asked, while he blotted the contract.

"I can start any time," I said a little uncertainly. "But shouldn't I rehearse first?"

He laughed. "You don't rehearse moving pictures in advance. You do that as they are being taken," he replied. "They'll show you all that at the studios. You'll soon catch on, and you'll photograph all right, don't worry."

Still with some misgivings, but becoming more jubilant every moment, I hurried away to get my luggage and to announce to Mr. Reeves that I was not going back to London with Karno's company. He began to urge me to change my mind, to wait while he could cable to Karno and get me an offer from him for the next season, but I triumphantly produced my contract, and after one look at the figures he was dumb.

"Two hundred dollars—Holy Moses!" he managed to ejaculate after a moment, and I chuckled at the thought of Mr. Karno's face when he should hear the news.

"It's not so bad, for a beginning," I said modestly, trying my best to speak as though it were but a trifle, but unable to keep the exultation out of my voice. A dozen times, in the hurry of arranging my affairs and catching the train, I stopped to look at the contract again, half fearful that the figures might have changed.

My high spirits lasted until I was settled in the Chicago Limited, pulling out of New York with a great noise of whistles and bells, and steaming away into the darkness toward California and the unknown work of a moving-picture actor. Then misgivings came upon me in a cloud. I saw myself trying to be funny before the cold eye of a machine, unable to speak my lines, not helped by any applause, failing miserably. How could I give the effect of ripping my trousers without the "r-r-r-r-rip!" of a snare-drum?[1] when I slipped and fell on my head, how could the audience get the point without the loud hollow "boom!" from the orchestra?

Every added mile farther from London increased my doubts, hard as I tried to encourage myself with thoughts of my past successes. Moving-picture work was different, and if I should fail in California I would be a long, long way from home.

I reached Los Angeles late at night, very glad that I would not have to report at the Keystone studios[2] until morning. I tried to oversleep next day, but it was impossible; I was awake long before dawn. I dressed as slowly as possible, wandered about the streets as long as I could, and finally ordered an enormous breakfast, choosing the most expensive cafe I could find, because the more expensive the place the longer one must wait to be served, and I was seizing every pretext for delay. When the food came I could not eat it, and suddenly I said to myself that I was behaving like a child; I would hurry to the studios and get it over. I rushed from the cafe, called a taxi and bribed the chauffeur to break the speed laws and get me there quick.

When I alighted before the studio, a big new building of bright unpainted wood, I took a deep breath, gripped my cane firmly, walked briskly to the door—and hurried past it. I walked a block or so, calling myself names, before I could bring myself to turn and come back. At last, with the feeling that I was dragging myself by the collar, I managed to get up the steps and push open the door.

117

I was welcomed with a cordiality that restored a little of my self-confidence. The director of the company in which I was to star had been informed of my arrival by telegraph and was waiting for me on the stage, they said. An office boy, whistling cheerfully, volunteered to take me to him, and, leading me through the busy offices, opened the stage door.

A glare of light and heat burst upon me. The stage, a yellow board floor covering at least two blocks, lay in a blaze of sunlight, intensified by dozens of white canvas reflectors stretched overhead. On it was a wilderness of "sets"—drawing-rooms, prison interiors, laundries, balconies, staircases, caves, fire-escapes, kitchens, cellars. Hundreds of actors were strolling about in costume; carpenters were hammering away at new sets; five companies were playing before five clicking cameras. There was a roar of confused sound—screams, laughs, an explosion, shouted commands, pounding, whistling, the bark of a dog. The air was thick with the smell of new lumber in the sun, flash-light powder, cigarette smoke.

The director was standing in his shirt-sleeves beside a clicking camera, holding a mass of manuscript in his hand and clenching an unlighted cigar between his teeth. He was barking short commands to the company which was playing—"To the left; to the left, Jim! There, hold it! Smile, Maggie! That's right. Good! Look out for the lamp!"

The scene over, he welcomed me cordially enough, but hurriedly.

"Glad to see you. How soon can you go to work? This afternoon? Good! Two o'clock, if you can make it. Look around the studio a bit, if you like. Sorry I haven't a minute to spare; I'm six hundred feet short this week, and they're waiting for the film. G'by. Two o'clock, sharp!" Then he turned away and cried, "All ready for the next scene. Basement interior," and was hard at work again.

**In which I see
a near-tragedy which
is a comedy on the films; meet
my fellow actors, the red and blue rats;
and prepare to fall through a trap-door with a pie.**

The little self-confidence I had been able to muster failed me entirely when the director dismissed me so crisply. The place was so strange to my experience, every one of the hundreds of persons about me was so absorbed in his work, barely glancing at me as I passed, that I felt helpless and out of place there. Still, the studio was crowded with interesting things to see, and I determined to remain and learn all I could of this novel business of producing cinema film before my own turn came to do it. So I assumed an air of dignity, marred somewhat by the fact that my collar was beginning to wilt and my nose burning red in the hot sunlight, and strolled down the stage behind the clicking cameras.

At a little distance I saw the front of a three-story tenement, built of brick, with windows and fire-escape all complete, looking quite natural in front, but supported by wooden scaffolding behind. Near it, on a high platform, was a big camera, and a man with a shade over his eyes busy adjusting it, and a dozen men were stretching a net such as acrobats use. A number of actors were hurrying in that direction, and I joined them, eager to see what was to happen.

"What's all the row?" I asked a girl in the costume of a nurse, who stood eating a sandwich, the only idle person in sight.

"Scene in a new comedy," she answered pleasantly but indifferently.

"Ah, yes. That's in my own line," I said importantly. "I am Charles Chaplin."

119

She looked at me, and I saw that she had never heard of me.

"You're a comedian?" she inquired.

"Yes," I answered sharply. "Er—do you go on in this?"

"Oh, no. I'm not an actress," she said, surprised. "I'm here professionally." I did not understand what she meant. "In case of accidents," she explained, plainly thinking me stupid. "Sometimes nothing happens, but you never can tell. Eight men were pretty badly hurt in the explosion in the comedy they put on last week," she finished brightly.

I felt a cold sensation creep up my spine.

In the "set" before us there was a great bustle of preparation. A long light ladder was set up at a sharp angle, firmly fastened at the bottom, but with the upper end unsupported, quivering in the air.

Men were running about shouting directions and questions. Suddenly, balancing precariously on the narrow platform behind the camera operator, the director appeared and clapped his hands sharply. "All ready down there?" he called.

"All ready!" some one yelled in reply.

"Let 'er go!"

The windows in the brick wall burst outward with a loud explosion and swirling clouds of smoke. Up the swaying ladder ran a policeman and at the same instant, caught up by invisible wires, another man soared through the air and met him. On the top rung of the ladder they balanced, clutching each other.

"Fight! Fight! Put some life into it!" yelled the director. "Turn on the water, Jim!"

My eyes straining in their sockets, I saw the two men in the air slugging each other desperately, while the ladder bent beneath them. Then from the ground a two-inch stream of water rose and struck them—held there, playing on them while they struggled.

"Great! Great! Keep it up!" the director howled. "More

smoke!" Another explosion answered him; through the eddying smoke I could see the two men still fighting, while the stream from the hose played on them.

"Let go now. Fall! Fall! I tell you, fall!" the director shouted. The two men lurched, the wires gave way, and, falling backward, sheer, from a height of twenty-five feet, the comedian dropped and struck the net. The net broke.

The scene broke up in a panic. The nurse ran through the crowd, a stretcher appeared, and on it the comedian was carried past me, followed by the troubled director and a physician. "Not serious, merely shock; he'll be all right to-morrow," the physician was saying, but I felt my knees shaking under me.

"So *this* is the life of a cinema comedian!" I thought, breathing hard.

I did not feel hungry, somehow, and besides, I felt that if I left the studio for luncheon I would probably be unable to bring myself back again, so I picked out the coolest place I could find and sat down to await two o'clock. I was in a dim damp "basement set," furnished only with an overturned box, on which I sat. After a time a strange scratching noise attracted my attention, and looking down I saw a procession of bright red and blue rats coming out between my feet. I leaped from the box with my hair on end and left, saying nothing to any one.

At two o'clock, quivering with nervousness, I presented myself to the director. He was brisk and hurried as before and plunged immediately into a description of the part I was to play, pausing only to mop his perspiring forehead now and then. The heat had increased; under the reflectors the place was like a furnace, but my spine was still cold with apprehension.

"Is it an acrobatic part?" I asked, as soon as I could force myself to inquire.

"No, not this one. You're a hungry tramp in the country.[1]

121

We'll take the interiors here, and for the rest we'll go out on 'location,' " the director answered, ruffling the pages of the "working script" of the play. "We'll do the last scene first— basement set. Let's run through it now; then you can make up and we'll get it on the film before the light's gone."

He led the way to the basement set and began to instruct me how to play the part.

"You fall in, down the trap-door," he said. "Pick yourself up, slowly, and register surprise. Don't look at the camera, of course. You have a pie under your coat. Take it out, begin to eat it. Register extreme hunger. Then you hear a noise, start, set down the pie, and peer out through the grating. When you turn around the rats will be eating the pie. Get it?"

I said I did, and while the director peered through the camera lens I rehearsed as well as I could. I had to do it over and over, because each time I forgot and got out of the range of the camera lens. At last, however, with the aid of a five-foot circle of dots on the floor, I did it passably well, and was sent to make up in one of dozens of dressing-rooms, built in a long row beside the stage. My costume, supplied by the Keystone wardrobe, was ready, and I was reassured by the sight of it and the make-up box. Here at last was something I was quite famil- iar with, and I produced a make-up of which I was proud.

When I returned to the stage the camera operator was waiting, and a small crowd of actors and carpenters had gathered to watch the scene. The director was inspecting the colored rats and giving orders to have their tails repainted— quick, because the blamed things had licked the color off and would register tailless. A stage hand was standing by with a large pie in his hand.

"Ready, Chaplin?" the director called, and then he looked at me.

"Holy Moses, where did you get that make-up?" he asked

in astonishment, and every one stared. "That won't do; that won't do at all. Look at your skin, man; it will register gray—and those lines—you can't use lines like that in the pictures. Roberts, go show him how to make up."

I thought of my first appearance in *From Rags to Riches*, and felt almost as humiliated as I had then, while Roberts went with me to the dressing-room and showed me how to coat my face and neck with a dull brick-brown paint, and to load my lashes heavily with black. The character lines I had drawn with such care would not do in the pictures, I learned, because they would show as lines. I must give the character effect by the muscles of my face.

Feeling very strange in this make-up, I went back the second time to the stage. The director, satisfied this time, gave me a few last directions and the pie, and I mounted to the top of the set.

"Remember, don't look at the camera, keep within range, throw yourself into the part and say anything that comes into your head," the director said. "All ready? Go to it."

The camera began to click; I clutched the pie, took a long breath, and tumbled through the trap-door.

**In which,
much against my will, I
eat three cherry pies; see myself for
the first time on a moving-picture screen and
discover that I am a hopeless failure on the films.**

"Register surprise!  Register surprise!"
the director ordered in a low voice, while
I struggled to get up without damaging
the pie. I turned my head toward the
clicking camera, and suddenly it seemed like a great eye watching me. I gazed into the round black lens, and it seemed to swell until it was yards across. I tried to pull my face into an expression of surprise, but the muscles were stiff and I could only stare fascinated at the lens. The clicking stopped.

"Too bad. You looked at the camera. Try it again," said the director, making a note of the number of feet of film spoiled. He was a very patient director; he stopped the camera and placed the pie on top of it for safety, while I fell through the trap-door twice and twice played the scene through, using the pie tin. Then the pie was placed under my coat again, the camera began to click, and again I started the scene. But the clicking drew my attention to the lens in spite of myself. I managed to keep from looking directly at it, but I felt that my acting was stiff, and half-way through the scene the camera stopped again.

"Out of range," said the camera man carelessly, and lighted a cigarette. I had forgotten the circle of dots on the floor and crossed them.

I had eaten a large piece of the pie. There was a halt while another was brought, and the director, after an anxious look at the sun, used the interval in playing the scene through himself, falling through the trap-door, registering surprise and apprehension and panic at the proper points, and impressing upon me the way it was done. Then I tried it again.

All that afternoon I worked, black and blue from countless falls on the cement floor, perspiring in the intense heat, and eating no less than three large pies, and I had never cared much for them at any time.

When the light failed that evening the director, with a troubled frown, thoughtfully folded the working script and dismissed the camera man. Most of the actors in the other companies had gone; the wilderness of empty sets looked weird in the shadows. A boy appeared, caught the rats by their tails, and popped them back into their box.

"Well, that's all for to-day. We'll try it again to-morrow," the director said, not looking at me. "I guess you'll get the hang of it all right, after a while."

In my dressing-room I scrubbed the paint from my face and neck with vicious rubs. I knew I had failed miserably and my self-esteem smarted at the thought. Even if I had succeeded, I said bitterly, what was the fun in a life like that? No excitement, no applause, just hard work all day and long empty evenings with nothing to do.

Only two considerations prevented me from canceling my contract and quitting at once—I was getting two hundred dollars a week, and I would not admit to myself that I—I, who had been a success with William Gillette and a star with Karno—was a failure in the films. Nevertheless, I was in a black mood that night, and when after dinner the waiter, bending deferentially at my elbow, insinuated politely, "The cherry pie is very good, sir," he fell back aghast at the language I used.

Work at the studio began at eight next morning, and I arrived very tired and ill-tempered because of waking so early. We began immediately on the same scene, and after I had ruined some more film by unexpectedly landing on a rat when I fell through the trap-door, we managed to get it done, to my relief. However, all that week, and the next, my troubles increased.

We played all the scenes which occurred in one set before we went on to the next set, so we were obliged to take the scenes at haphazard through the play, with no continuity or apparent connection. The interiors were all played on the stage, and most of the exteriors were taken "on location," that is, somewhere in the country. It was confusing, after being booted through a door, to be obliged to appear on the other side of it two days later, with the same expression, and complete the tumble begun fifteen miles away. It was still more confusing to play the scenes in reverse order, and I ruined three hundred feet of film by losing my hat at the end of a scene, when the succeeding one had already been played with my hat on.

At the end of the second week the comedy was all on the film and the director and I were being polite to each other with great effort. I was angry with every one and everything, my nerves worn thin with the early hours and unaccustomed work, and he was worried because I had made him a week late in producing the film. The day the negative was done Mack Sennett arrived from New York, and I met him with a jauntiness which was a hollow mockery of my real feeling.

"Well, they tell me the film's done," he said heartily, shaking my hand. "Now you're going to see yourself as others see you for the first time. Is the dark room ready? Let's go and see how you look on the screen."

The director led the way, and the three of us entered a tiny perfectly dark room. I could hear my heart beating while we waited, and talked nervously to cover the sound of it. Then there was a click, the shutter opened, and the picture sprang out on the screen. It was the negative, which is always shown before the real film is made, and on it black and white were reversed. It was several seconds before I realized that the black-face man in white clothes, walking awkwardly before me, was myself. Then I stared in horror.

126

Funny? A blind man couldn't have laughed at it. I had ironed out entirely any trace of humor in the scenario. It was stiff, wooden, stupid. We sat there in silence, seeing the picture go on, seeing it become more awkward, more constrained, more absurd with every flicker. I felt as though the whole thing were a horrible nightmare of shame and embarrassment. The only bearable thing in the world was the darkness; I felt I could never come out into the light again, knowing I was the same man as the inane ridiculous creature on the film. Half-way through the picture Mr. Sennett took pity on me and stopped the operator.

"Well, Chaplin, you didn't seem to get it that time," he said. "What's wrong, do you suppose?"

"I don't know," I said.

"Yes, it's plain we can't release this," the director put in moodily. "Two thousand feet of film spoiled."

"Oh, damn your film!" I burst out in a fury, and rising with a spring which upset my chair I slammed open the door and stalked out. "Well, here is where I quit the pictures," I thought.

Mr. Sennett and the director overtook me before I reached my dressing-room and we talked it over. I felt that I would never make a moving-picture actor, but Mr. Sennett was more hopeful. "You're a crackerjack comedian," he said. "And you'll photograph well. All you need is to get camera-wise. We'll try you out in something else; I'll direct you, and you will get the hang of the work all right."

The director brought out a mass of scenarios which had been passed up to him by the scenario department and Mr. Sennett picked out one and ordered the working script of it made immediately. Next day we set to work together on it; Mr. Sennett patient, good-humored, considerate, coaching me over and over in every gesture and expression; I with a hard tense determination to make a success this time.

We worked another week on this second play, using every

127

hour of good daylight. It was not entirely finished then, but enough was done to give an idea of its success, and again the negative was sent to the dark room for review.

I went to see it with the sensations of dread and shrinking one feels at sight of a dentist's chair, and my worst fears wre justified. The film was worse than the first one—utterly stupid and humorless.

In which I
introduce an innovation
in motion-picture production;
appropriate an amusing mustache; and
wager eighty dollars on three hours' work.

"Well, what are we go-  ing to do about it?"
Mr. Sennett asked, when the flicker of
the second film had ceased and we knew it
a worse failure than the first. "Looks hopeless, doesn't it?"

"Yes," I said, with a sinking heart, for after all I had had a
flicker of hope for success this time. We had both worked hard,
and now we were tired and discouraged. I went alone to my
dressing-room, shut the door and sat down to think it over.

The trouble with the films, I decided, was lack of spontaneity. I was stiff; I took all the surprise out of the scenes by anti-
cipating the next motion. When I walked against a tree, I showed that I knew I would hit it, long before I did. I was so determined to be funny that every muscle in my body was stiff
and serious with the strain. And then that confounded clicking
of the camera and the effort it took to keep from looking at
it—and the constant fear of spoiling a foot of film.

"So you're a failure," I said, looking at myself in the mirror. "You're a failure, no good; down and out. You can't make
a cinema film. You're beaten by a click and an inch of celluloid.
You *are* a rotter, no mistake!"

I was so furious at that that I smashed the mirror into bits
with my fist. I walked up and down the dressing-room, hating
myself and the camera and the film and the whole detestable
business. I thought of haughtily stalking out and telling Mr.
Sennett I was through with the whole thing; I was going back
to London, where I was appreciated. Then I knew he would
be glad to let me go; he would say to himself that I was no good

in the pictures, and I would always know it was true. My vanity ached at the thought. No matter how much success I made, no matter how loud the audience applauded, I would always say to myself, "Very well for you, but you know you failed in the cinemas."

With a furious gesture I grabbed my hat and went out to find Mr. Sennett. He was on the stage watching the work of another company. I walked up to him in a sort of cold rage and said, "See here, Mr. Sennett, I can succeed in this beastly work. I know I can. You let me have a chance to do things the way I want to and I'll show you."

"I don't know what I can do. You've had the best scenarios we've got, and we haven't hurried you," he said reasonably. "You know the rest of the companies get out two reels a week, and we've taken three weeks to do what we've done with you— about a reel and a half."

"Yes, but the conditions are all wrong," I hurried on. "Rehearsing over and over, and no chance to vary an inch, and then that clicking beginning just when I start to play. And I miss a cane. I have to have a cane to be funny."

It must have sounded childish enough. Mr. Sennett looked at me in surprise.

"You can have a cane, if that's what you want. But I don't know how you are going to make pictures without rehearsing and without a camera," he said.

"I want to make up my own scenarios as I go along. I just want to go out on the stage and be funny," I said. "And I want the camera to keep going all the time, so I can forget about it."

"Oh, see here, Chaplin, you can't do that. Do you know what film costs? Four cents a foot, a thousand feet of film. You'd waste thousands of dollars' worth of it in a season. You see that yourself. Great Scott, man, you can't take pictures that way!"

CHARLIE CHAPLIN'S OWN STORY

"You give me a chance at it, and I'll show you whether I can or not," I replied. "Let me try it just for a day or so, just one scene. If the film's spoiled, I'll pay for it myself."

We argued it out for a long time. The notion seemed utterly crazy to Mr. Sennett, but after all I had made a real success in comedy, and his disappointment must have been great at my failure on the films. Finally he consented to let me try making pictures my way, on condition that I should pay the salary of the operator and the cost of the spoiled film.

That night I walked up and down the street for hours, planning the outlines of a scenario and the make-up I would wear. My cane, of course, and the loose baggy trousers which are always funny on the stage,[1] I don't know why. I debated a long time about the shoes. My feet are small, and I thought perhaps they might seem funnier in tight shoes, under the baggy trousers. At last, however, I decided on the long, flat, floppy shoes, which would trip me up unexpectedly.

These details determined upon, I was returning to my hotel when suddenly I discovered I was hungry, and remembered that I had eaten no dinner. I dropped into a cafeteria for a cup of coffee, and there I saw a mustache. A little clipped mustache, worn by a very dignified solemn gentleman who was eating soup. He dipped his spoon into the bowl and the mustache quivered apprehensively. He raised the spoon and the mustache drew back in alarm. He put the soup to his lips and the mustache backed up against his nose and clung there.

It was the funniest thing I had ever seen. I choked my coffee, gasped, finally laughed outright. I must have a mustache like that!

Next day, dressed in the costume I had chosen, I glued the mustache to my lip before the dressing-room mirror, and shouted at the reflection. It was funny; it was uproariously funny! It waggled when I laughed, and I laughed again. I went out

131

on the stage still laughing, and followed by a shout of mirth from every one who saw me. I tripped on my cane, fell over my shoes, got the camera man shouting with mirth. A crowd collected to watch me work, and I plunged into my first scene in high spirits.

I played the scene over and over, introducing funnier effects each time. I enjoyed it thoroughly, stopping every time I got out of the range of the camera to laugh again. The other actors, watching behind the camera, held their sides and howled, as my old audiences had done when I was with Karno. "This," I said to myself triumphantly. "This is going to be a success!"

When the camera finally stopped clicking all my old self-confidence and pride had come back to me. "Not so bad, what?" I said, triumphantly twirling my cane, and in sheer good spirits I pretended to fall against the camera, wringing a shout of terror from the operator. Then, modestly disclaiming the praises of the actors, though indeed I felt they were less than I deserved, I went whistling to my dressing-room.

"How soon do you want to see the film, Mr. Chaplin?" the operator asked, tapping at my door while I was changing into street clothes.

"Just as soon as you can have it, old top," I replied cheerfully. "Oh, by the way, how many feet did we use?"

"Little over two thousand," he called back, and I heard the sound of his retreating feet.

A little over two thousand! At four cents a foot! Eighty dollars! I felt as though a little cold breeze was blowing on my back. Nearly a month's salary with Karno wagered on the success of three hours' work! After all, I thought, I was not sure how the film would turn out; the beastly machine might not see the humor of my acting, good as it had been. I finished dressing in a hurry, and went out to find Mr. Sennett and show him the film in the dark room.

I sat on the edge of my chair in the dark room, waiting for the picture to flash on the screen, thinking of that eighty dollars, which alternately loomed large as a fortune and sank into insignificance. If the picture was good—. But suppose it, too, was a failure! Then I would be stranded in California, thousands of miles from home, and where would I get the eighty dollars?

The shutter clicked open and the negative began to flicker on the screen. I saw myself, black-faced, with a little white mustache and enormous white shoes, walking in great dignity across the patch of light. I saw myself trip over my shoes. I saw the mustache quiver with alarm. I saw myself stop, look wise, twirl my cane knowingly, and hit myself on the nose. Then, suddenly in the stillness, I heard a loud chuckle from Mr. Sennett. The picture was good. It was very good.

"Well, Chaplin, you've done it! By George, you've certainly got the comedy! It's a corker!" Mr. Sennett said, clapping me heartily on the back as we came out of the dark room. "You've wasted a lot of film, but hang the film! You're worth it! Go on and finish this up. I'd like to release it next week."

In which I taste
success in the movies; develop a
new aim in life; and form an ambitious project.

"We'll use the third **29** scene," Mr. Sennett said to the camera operator. "How long will it run?"

"About two hunerator replied. dred feet," the op-

"Well, keep it and throw away the rest. Think you can finish two good reels this week?" Mr. Sennett asked, turning to me.

"Watch me!" I responded airily, and my heart gave a great jump. They were paying me two hundred dollars a week and were willing to throw away thousands of feet of film in addition to get my comedies. "There's a fortune in this business! A fortune!" I thought.

My ambition soared at that moment to dazzling heights. I saw myself retiring, after five or ten years in the business, with a fortune of ten thousand pounds—yes even twenty thousand!

The comedy was finished that week; I worked every day, during every moment when the light was good, not stopping for luncheon or to rest. I enjoyed the work; the even click-click-click of the camera, running steadily, was a stimulant to me; my ideas came thick and fast. I sketched in my mind the outlines of a dozen comedies, to be played later. I remembered all the funny things I had seen or heard and built up rough scenarios around them. I woke in the night, chuckling at a new idea that occurred to me.

When my first comedy was released it was a great success. The producers demanded more, quickly. I was already working on *Caught in the Rain*. I followed it the next week with *Laughing Gas*.[1] They all went big.

Every morning when I reached the stage in make-up the actors who were to play with me stood waiting to learn what their parts were to be. I myself did not always know, but when I had limbered up a bit by a jig or clog dance and the camera began to click, ideas came fast enough.

I told the other actors how to play their parts, played them myself to show how it should be done; played my own part enthusiastically, teased the camera man, laughed and whistled and turned handsprings. The clicking camera took it all in; later, in the negative room, we chose and cut and threw away film, picking out the best scenes, rearranging the reels, shaping up the final picture to be shown on the screens. I liked it all; I was never still a minute in the studio and never tired.

The only time I was quiet was while I was making up. Then I thought sometimes of my early days in England, of Covent Garden, and my mother and my year with William Gillette. "Life's a funny thing," I said to myself. Then I made up as a baker, ordered a wagonload of bread-dough and flour and went out and romped through it hilarious, shouting with laughter whenever I was out of range of the camera. The result was *Dough and Dynamite*,[2] and it clinched what I then thought was my success in the movies.

At first when my pictures began to appear in the moving-picture houses I took great delight in walking among the crowds in front of the doors, idly twirling my cane and listening to the comments on my comedies. I liked to go inside, too, and hear the audiences laugh at the comical figure I cut on the screen. That was the way I got my first real ambition in moving-picture work. I still have it. I want to make people chuckle.

Audiences laugh in two ways. Up on the stage, in all the tense effort of being funny behind the footlights, I had never noticed that. But one night, packed with the crowd in a small, dark moving-picture house, watching the flickering screen, listening for the response of the people around me, I suddenly realized it.

I had wedged into a crowded house to see my latest film. It was a rough-and-tumble farce; the audience had been holding its sides and shrieking hysterically for five minutes. "Oh, ho!" I was saying to myself. "You're gettin 'em, old top, you're getting 'em!" Suddenly the laughter stopped.

I looked around dismayed. I could see a hundred faces, white in the dim light, intent on the picture—and not a smile on any of them. I looked anxiously at the screen. There was Charlie Chaplin in his make-up standing still. Standing still in a farce! I wondered how I had ever let a thing like that get past the negative. The house was still; I could hear the click of the unrolling film.

Then on the screen I saw myself turn slowly; saw my expression become grim and resolute; saw myself grip my cane firmly and stalk away. I was going after the husky laborer who had stolen my beer.

Then it came—a chuckle, a deep hearty "Ha! Ha! Ha!" It spread over the crowd like a wave; the house rocked with it.

"That's it! That's what I want, that's what I want!" I said. I got out quickly to think it over. I had to crowd past the knees of a dozen people to do it, and not one of them glared at me. They were still chuckling.

I walked back to my hotel with my cane tucked under my arm and my hands in my pockets. That was the thing—the chuckle! Any kind of laughter is good; any kind of laughter will get the big salaries. But a good, deep, hearty chuckle is the thing that warms a man's heart; it's the thing that makes him your friend; it's the thing that shows, when you get it, that you have a real hold on your audience. I have worked for it ever since.

After that I visited the picture houses night after night,

watching for that chuckle, planning ways to get it. I was never recognized by strangers, and more than once some one asked me what I thought of Charlie Chaplin. I do not recall that I ever told the truth. In fact, I was not thinking much about Charlie Chaplin in those days; I was thinking of his work and his success and his growing bank-account.

I had come into the business at the height of its first big success. Fortunes were being made overnight in it; producers could not turn out film fast enough to satisfy the clamoring public. The studios were like gambling houses in the wild fever of play. Money was nothing; it was thrown away by hundreds, by thousands. "Give us the film, give us the film! To hell with the expense!" was the cry. I heard of small tailors, of street-car motormen, who had got into the game with a few hundred dollars and now were millionaires. In six months I was smiling at my early notion of making fifty thousand dollars.

Sydney, who was still in vaudeville, came to Los Angeles about that time, and I met him at the train with one of the company's big automobiles. The same old reliable Sydney with his sound business sense. He had figured out the trend of affairs and was already negotiating with the Essanay company for a good contract with them, going deliberately into the work I had blundered into by accident.

"There's a fortune in this if it's handled right, Charlie," he said.

"A fortune? If this holds out, if I can keep up my popularity, I'll have a cool half million before I quit, my lad! Keep your eye piped[3] for your Uncle Charlie!" I said gaily.

**In which I see myself as others see me;
learn many surprising things about myself
from divers sources; and see a bright future ahead.**

Syd laughed. "Well, have it your way, old top!" he said. "What will you do when you get your half million?"

"Do? I'll quit. I'll be satisfied," I said. "You can't keep 'em coming forever, and I don't expect it. I'll give them the best I have as long as I can, and then—curtains! But I wager we keep out of the Actor's Home, what?"

Syd laughed again. "There's money in the movies, Charlie," he said. "Half a million? You wait a year. Your popularity hasn't begun."

He was right. In a world where so many people are troubled and unhappy, where women lead such dreary lives as my mother did when I was a boy, where men spend their days in hard unwilling toil and children starve as I starved in the London slums, laughter is precious. People want to laugh; they long to forget themselves for half an hour in the hearty joy of it. Every night on a hundred thousand motion-picture screens my floppy shoes and tricky cane and eloquent mustache were making people laugh, and they remembered them and came to laugh again. Suddenly, almost overnight, Charlie Chaplin became a fad, a craze.

My first idea of it came one night when I was returning from a hard day's work at the studio. It had been a hot day; I had worked thirteen hours in a mask of grease paint under the blazing heat of the Southern California sun intensified by a dozen huge reflectors before the inexorable click-click-click of the camera, driven by the necessity of finishing the reel while the light lasted. My exuberance of spirit had waned by noon; by

138

four o'clock I was driving myself by sheer will-power, doggedly, determinedly being funny. At seven we finished the reel. At nine we had got the film in shape in the negative room, and I had nothing to do till next morning but get my ideas together for a new comedy.

I was slumped in a heap in the tonneau of the director's car hurrying to my hotel and thinking that the American system of built-in baths had its advantages, when we ran up to a crowd that almost stopped street traffic. The sidewalk was jammed for half a block; men were standing up in automobiles to get a better view of whatever was happening. My chauffeur stopped.

"What's the row?" I asked one of the men in the crowd.

"Charlie Chaplin's in there!" he said excitedly, jumping on the running-board and craning his neck to look over the heads of the men in front of him.

"Really?" I said. I stood up and looked. There in front of a moving-picture theater was Charlie Chaplin, sure enough— shoes, baggy trousers, mustache and all. The chap was walking up and down as well as he could in the jam of people, twirling his cane and tripping over his shoes. Policemen were trying to clear the sidewalk, but the crowd was mad for a glimpse of him. I stood there looking at him with indescribable emotions.

"That's funny," I said after a minute. The man on the running-board had only half heard me.

"Funny? I should say he is! He's the funniest man in America!" he said. "They say he gets a hundred dollars a day and only works when he's stewed."

"Well, well! Really!" I said.

"I guess that's right, too," he went on. "He acts like it on the screen, don't he? Say, have you seen his latest picture? Man, it's a knockout! When he fell into that sewer—! They faked the sewer, of course, but say—! I like to of fell out of my seat!"

We had not faked the sewer. It was a thoroughly real sewer. But I drove on to my hotel without explaining. The whole situation was too complex.

Within a week half the motion-picture houses in Los Angeles had the only original and genuine Charlie Chaplin parading up and down before them. I grew so accustomed to meeting myself on the street that I started in surprise every time I looked into a mirror without my make-up. Overnight, too, a thousand little figures of Charlie Chaplin[1] in plaster sprang up and crowded the shop windows. I could not buy a tooth-brush without reaching over a counter packed with myself to do it.

It was odd, walking up and down the streets, eating in cafés, hearing Charlie Chaplin talked about, seeing Charlie Chaplin on every hand and never being recognized as Charlie Chaplin. I had a feeling that all the world was crosseyed, or that I was a disembodied spirit. But that did not last long. A plague of reporters descended on the studios soon, like whatever it was that fell upon Egypt. Then the world seemed more topsy-turvy than ever, for here I was, an actor, dodging reporters!

Not that I have any dislike of reporters. Indeed, in the old days I asked nothing better than to get one to listen to me and often planned for days to capture one's attention. But that's another of life's little jokes. A man who tries hard enough for anything will always get it—after he has stopped wanting it.

I had to turn out the film, hundreds of feet of it every week, and it must be made while the light lasted. The gambling fever had spent itself in the picture business; directors were beginning to count costs. To stop my company half an hour meant a waste of several hundred dollars. And every morning half a dozen reporters waited for me to give them "Just a few minutes, Mr. Chaplin!"

I took to dodging in and out of the studio like a hunted

man. Did I stop to give a harried and unwary opinion upon something I knew nothing whatever about, next Sunday I beheld with staring eyes a full-page story on my early life, told in the first person. At last, in the pressure of getting out two new comedies in a hurry, I escaped interviews for nearly three weeks. We were working overtime; it was late in the fall, when the weather was uncertain and the light bad. We would start at five in the morning to get to our "location" in the country by sunrise, only to have the morning foggy. Then we hurried back to the studio to work under artificial light, and the afternoon was sunny. It was a hard nerve-racking three weeks and our tempers were not improved when, at the end of the last day, we tried out the negative as usual and found the camera had leaked light and ruined nearly a reel of film.

Hurrying off the stage to get a quick supper, so that I could return and make up as much lost time as possible that night, I encountered on the studio steps a thin young man in a derby, who did not recognize me.

"Say, is it true Chaplin's crazy?" he asked.

"Crazy?" I said.

"Yes. He hasn't released a film for over a month and I can't get hold of him here. They say he's raving crazy, confined in an asylum.

"He is not," I said. Then the humor of the thing struck me. "He isn't violent yet," I said, "but he may be, any minute."

Half an hour later two morning papers telephoned the director for confirmation of the report, which he denied emphatically and profanely. No story appeared in the papers, but I have since been solemnly told by a hundred prople who "have it straight" that Chaplin is, or has been, confined in the California Hospital for the Insane.

Behind all this flurry of comment and conjecture I was working, working hard, turning out the best film I could devise, with my mind always on the problem of getting that deep, hearty chuckle from the audience. I did not always get it, but I did get laughs. And my contract with the Keystone company was running out; I saw still brighter prospects ahead.

**In which
the moving-picture
work palls on me; I make other
plans, am persuaded to abandon them
and am brought to the brink of a deal in high finance.**

The reorganization of motion pictures, era of mushroom overnight, making **31** among the producers which followed the companies sprung up fabulous fortunes, wildly, in the first scramble for quick profits and going down again in the general chaos, was still under way when my contract with the Keystone company expired.

Millions of laughs, resounding every night in hundreds of moving-picture theaters had set producers to bidding for me. I received offers of incredible sums from some companies; lavish promises of stock from others. The situation, I felt, required the mind of a financier. I call in Sydney.[1]

After a great deal of consideration, we decided to accept the offer of the Essanay company,[2] as combining in due proportion size of salary and security of its payment. My contract called for a thousand dollars a day, also a percentage on my films.

A thousand dollars a day! Two hundred pounds every twenty-four hours! At the moment of signing the contract a feeling of unreality came over me. It seemed incredible. Only five years ago I had been cockily congratulating myself on wringing ten pounds a week from Karno!

I returned to Los Angeles in the highest spirits and set to work again. A small company, three actors and a score of "supers," was got together for me. The stage, a rough board structure large enough for a dozen "sets," built near the bridge of the street railway between Los Angeles and Pasadena, was turned over to me and my company. Here, on a little side street

143

of tumble-down sheds half buried in tangles of dusty woods, I shut myself in behind the high wooden wall of the studio through the long hot summer and worked at being funny.

Every morning, as soon as the light was right for the pictures, I arrived at the studio and got into my make-up, racking my brain the while for a funny idea. The company stood waiting in the white-hot glare of the big canvas reflectors; the camera was ready; at the other end of the long-distance wire the company clamored for film, more film and still more. I must go out on the stage and be funny, be funny as long as the light lasted.

"The whole thing's in your hands, Chaplin," the managers said cheerfully. "Give us the film, that's all we ask."

I gave them the film. All day long, tumbling down-stairs, falling into lakes, colliding with moving vans, upsetting stepladders, sitting in pails of wall-paper paste, I heard it click-click-clicking past the camera shutter. At night, in the negative room, I checked and cut and revised it. And all the time I searched my mind for funny ideas.

Now, nothing in the world is more rare than an idea, except a funny idea. The necessity of working out a new one every day, the responsibility of it and the labor so wore upon me that by fall I had come to a stern determination. I would leave the moving pictures. I would leave them as soon as I had a million dollars.

"If this keeps up another year I will be a millionaire," I said to myself one evening, lying on the cement floor of the basement set, where I had gone in my search for a cool spot to rest. "Then I'll quit. I will quit and write a book. I never have written a book, and I might as well. But not a funny book. Ye gods, no!"

After all, I had had my share of the limelight, as I had always known, even in my worst days, that I would some day. I had made my success on the legitimate stage with William Gillette. I had made my success and my money in the moving pictures in America. I was still in my twenties. Why not leave the stage altogether, settle down on some snug little ranch and write? It might be jolly fun to be an author. By jove, I'd do it!

My arrangement with the Essanay people had been for only a year—Sydney's prudent idea. The contract was expiring in a few months; already I was receiving offers from other companies. I would refuse them all; yes, I would quit with less than a million dollars. Three-quarters of a million would be plenty. Lying there on the cool cement floor, still in my baggy trousers, with the grease paint on my face, I stretched my legs and waggled my floppy shoes contentedly. Jove, the relief of never being funny again!

"Charlie, old boy, don't be a gory idiot!" Syd protested, when I told him my project. "Why, you can make a fortune at this. Hutchinson, of the Mutual,[3] is in town right now; I was talking to him last night. They'll make you an offer—you can get fifty offers that will beat anything you've dreamed about. You can be the highest-paid movie actor in the world."

"What's a million more or less, old man?" I said airily, though I began to waver. "I've made my pile. I want to write a book."

"How do you know you can write a book?" Sydney returned. "Of all the bally rot! D'you want to go off somewhere and never be heard of again? Or have you got another notion that William Gillette's going to take you to America?"

It was the first time Sydney had ever mentioned that affair since the day he had bought me clothes and so got me out of the London hospital and taken me home. I had told him all about it then.

It struck me he was probably right. It has been my experience that he usually is.

145

"All right," I said. "Your contract's up with the Essanay, too. Come over and manage things for me and I'll stay with the moving pictures."

He agreed and we began to consider which company I should choose. The moving-picture business is standardized now; a few big companies practically divide the field between them. The various departments of the work have been segregated also, a producing company turning its films over to a releasing company which markets them. What we most desired was to make a connection with a big releasing company, since if I got a percentage of the profits which we meant to stand out for, the marketing of the films was most important.

I felt greatly relieved when my contract expired and I drove away from the studio for the last time, free for some weeks from the obligation of being funny. Sydney was busily negotiating with several companies, considering their offers and their advantages from our view-point. I was idle and carefree; I might do what I liked. I whistled cheerfully to myself, swinging my cane as I walked down to dinner that night, facing the prospect before me with happy anticipation.

In a week I discovered that the one thing I most wanted to do was to be acting. A thousand bright ideas for comedy situations rushed into my mind; I longed to put on my make-up again, to smell the piny odor of the studio in the hot sun, to hear the click of the camera. I looked regretfully at the old signs on the movie theaters; no new Chaplin pictures were being released. I was eager to be back at work.

Each night I discussed more eagerly with Sydney the different companies we were considering. At last, after a great many talks with Mr. Hutchinson, we privately decided on the Mutual as offering the best advantages. This decision, however, we prudently refrained from mentioning until after Mr. Caulfield,[4] the personal representative of the Mutual's president, Mr. Freuler,[5] should come to Los Angeles and make us a definite money offer.

Mr. Caulfield promptly arrived, and Sydney undertook the negotiations with him, keeping me in reserve to bring up at the proper time. I relied a great deal upon Sydney; I knew myself entirely capable in handling theatrical managers, but I had greater confidence in Sydney's handling of business men. I awaited somewhat nervously my share in the arrangements.

One night my cue came. Sydney telephoned up from down-stairs. "I'm bringing Caulfield up," he said. "He offers ten thousand a week and royalties. I'm holding out for two hundred and fifty thousand dollars bonus on signing the contract. Stick at that if you can, but whatever you do, don't take less than one hundred and twenty-five thousand dollars."

In which I see success in my grasp; proudly consider the heights to which I have climbed; and receive an unexpected shock.

Sydney came in a moment later, bringing Mr. Caulfield. Like Mr. Hutchinson, like, indeed, most of the men handling the affairs of the big motion-picture corporations, Mr. Caulfield is a keen, quick-witted business man. Producing and selling moving-picture films is now a business as matter of fact as dealing in stocks and bonds; there is nothing of the theatrical manager about the men who control it.

"Well, Mr. Chaplin, your brother and I have been reaching an agreement about your contract with us," he said briskly. "We will give you a salary of ten thousand dollars a week and royalties that should double that figure." He mentioned the per cent agreed upon, as I assented.

"More than that, we are planning to create a separate producing company, subsidiary to the Mutual, which will be its releasing company, and to call the new concern the Lone Star company[1]—you to be the lone star. The new company will build its own studios at Santa Barbara, and it will give you the finest supporting cast that money can hire." He mentioned a few of the actors he had in mind, and I agreed heartily to his suggestions. They were good actors; I knew I could do good work with them.

"That is the offer as it stands," he concluded. "Half a million dollars in salary, another half-million, probably, in royalties. That depends on the amount of film the Lone Star company turns out. We'll give you every facility for producing it; the Mutual will handle the releases. We will be ready to start work as soon as you sign the contract."

"Then," I said pleasantly, "we need only decide the amount of the bonus to be paid me for signing it."

"Frankly, Mr. Chaplin, I am not authorized to offer you a bonus," he replied. "We don't do that. And we feel that in organizing your own company, building studios, giving you such a supporting cast, we are doing all that is possible, in addition to the record-breaking salary and royalties we are willing to pay you."

"On the other hand, you must consider that I have other offers," I answered. "Frankly, also, I imagine the size of the bonus paid me will decide which company I choose. I want two hundred and fifty thousand. We both know I am worth it to any company."

It was a deadlock. The old thrill of my dealing with Karno came back to me while we talked. In the end he left, the matter still undecided.

There were many interviews after that. I still believe that it might have been possible, by holding out longer, to get that amount, but I was eager to begin work again, and besides, as Mr. Caulfield pointed out, the sooner we began releasing films the sooner the royalties would begin coming in.

In the end we compromised on a cash bonus of one hundred and fifty thousand dollars, and an agreement on my part to secure the company for that payment by allowing them to insure my life for half a million dollars. We made application for the insurance policy and I was examined by the insurance company's physician, so that there might be no delay in closing the arrangements with the Mutual and beginning work.

"Fit as a fiddle, sir; fit as a fiddle!" the doctor said, thumping my chest. He felt the muscles of my arms approvingly. "Outdoor life, outdoor life and exercise, they're the best medicine in the world. What is your occupation, sir, if I may ask?"

"I'm a sort of rough-and-tumble acrobat," I said. "A moving-picture actor."

"Well, bless my soul! Chaplin, of course! I didn't get the name. Yes, yes, I see the resemblance now. I'm glad to meet you, sir. That last comedy of yours—when you fell into the lake—" He chuckled.

In great good spirits, then, we set out for New York, where the contract was to be signed by Mr. Freuler and myself and the final details settled.

Ten years ago I had been a starving actor on the Strand, a precocious youngster with big dreams and an empty stomach. Now I was on my way to New York and a salary of five hundred and twenty thousand dollars a year. Then I had been hungry for the slightest recognition; I had schemed and posed and acted a part with every one I met, craving a glance of admiration or envy to encourage my really tremulous hopes of one day succeeding; I had deceived myself with flattery to keep up my spirits. Now my name was known wherever moving pictures were shown throughout the world; a million hearty laughs applauded me every day.

I felt that I had arrived and I was happy.

From New York I hastened to cable my mother the dazzling news—my poor, pretty little mother, older now and never really strong since the terrible days when we starved together in a London garret. She can not come to America because she can not stand the sea trip,[2] but from the first I had written her at great length about my tremendous success, and when my comedies appeared in England she went for the first time to the cinema houses, and wrote that it was good to see me again and my comedy work was splendid; she was proud of me.

We were to sign the contract in the offices of the Mutual company in New York. When we stepped into that suite of richly furnished rooms, to be ushered at once into the presence of the president of this multi-million-dollar parent corporation, I had one fleeting thought of myself, ten years before, wearily tramping the Strand from agent's office to agent's office, the scorn of the grimiest cockney office boy.

The curious twists and turns of chance in those old days should have prepared me for the shock I received when I met Mr. Freuler, but they had not done so. I felt so secure, so satisfied with myself and the world as I stepped into his private office.

"I'm sorry, Mr. Chaplin," he said when Mr. Caulfield had introduced us and we were seated. "I'm afraid there will be a hitch in the paying of that bonus. The insurance company has refused to issue your policy."

In which I realize my wildest dreams of fortune; ponder on the comedy tricks of life and conclude without reaching any conclusion.

"Refused to issue— starting in my chair. a knife stab I saw the very moment of **33** impossible!" I cried, With the swiftness of myself stopped at my greatest success, fighting, struggling, hoping—and dying swiftly of some inexorable, concealed disease. Why, I had never felt better in my life!

"Yes, we received their refusal only this morning. On account of your extra-hazardous occupation they will not carry a policy for such a large sum," said Mr. Freuler. "I'm sorry, but I'm afraid it will hold matters up until we have found a company which will insure you or distributed the amount among a number of companies."

I laughed. I felt that Fate had shot her last bolt at me and missed. Extra-hazardous, of course! I had grown accustomed to the staff of nurses waiting at every large studio during thrilling scenes. I had trained myself by long practise to come comically through every dangerous mishap with as little danger of broken bones as possible. That was part of the work of being funny.

"Oh, very well," I said. "What shall we do to arrange the matter?"

It was a question which occupied our thoughts for several days. No large company would insure my life against the hazards of my comedies. We did, however, finally hit upon a way of solving the problem, and at last, worth nearly half a million dollars to the Mutual company if I died and much more if I lived, I signed the contract and received my check for one hundred and fifty thousand dollars.

I did it, as was fitting, to the sound of a clicking camera, for the Mutual company, with great enterprise, filmed the event, that audiences the world over might see me in my proper person, wielding the fateful pen. It was a moment during which I should have felt a degree of emotion, that moment at which the pen point, scrawling "Charles Chaplin," made me worth another million dollars. But the click-click-click of the camera as the operator turned the crank made the whole thing unreal to me. I was careful only to register the proper expression.

"Well—it's finished. What about your half-million now?" Sydney said affectionately when, my copy of the contract safely tucked into my breast pocket, we set off down the street together. "You'll quit, will you, with half a million! You'll never leave the moving pictures, my lad!"

"Have it your own way, old scamp," I said. "You would, anyway. Just the same I would like to write a book. I wager I could do it, with half a chance. By the way, there's another thing I'd like to do—"

Then I had all the pleasure and delight of feeling rich, of which the camera had robbed me while I signed my contract. At last I had an opportunity to repay Sydney the money part of the debt I have owed him since he came to my rescue so many times when we were boys. He could not refuse half of the bonus money which he had worked so hard to get for me, and that check for seventy-five thousand dollars gave me more pleasure than I can recall receiving from any other money I have ever handled.

So I came back to the Pacific coast to begin my work with the Mutual company. I am now an assured success in moving-picture comedy work and I am most proud of it. There is great cause for pride in keeping thousands of persons laughing. There is the satisfaction, also, of having attained, through lucky chance and accident, the goal on which I set my eyes so many years ago.

But I have no golden rule for such attainment to offer any one. I have worked—yes, to the limit of my ability—but so have many other men who have won far less reward than I. Whether you call it chance, fate or providence, to my mind the ruling of men's lives is in other hands than theirs.

If Sydney had not returned to London I might have become a thief in the London streets. If William Gillette had brought me to America I might have become a great tragic actor. If the explosion in the glass factory had been more violent I might have been buried in a pauper's grave. Now, by a twist of public fancy, which sees great humor in my best work, and less in the best work of other men who are toiling as hard as I, I have become Charlie Chaplin, "the funniest man in America," and a millionaire.

What rules our destinies in this big comedy, the world? I do not know. I know only that it is good, whatever happens, to laugh at it.

Meantime, I am working on a new comedy. I am always working on a new comedy. I have a whole stage to myself, a stage of bare new boards that smell of turpentine in the hot sunshine, covered with dozens of sets—drawing-rooms, bedrooms, staircases, basements, roofs, fire-escapes, laundries, baker-shops, barrooms—everything.

As soon as the light is strong enough I arrive in my big automobile, falling over the steps when I get out to amuse the chauffeur.[1] I coat my face with light brown paint, paste on my mustache, get into my floppy shoes, loop my trousers up about my waist, clog-dance a bit. Then the camera begins to click and I begin to be funny. I enjoy my comedies; they seem the funniest things on earth while I am playing them. I laugh, the other actors laugh, the director fans himself with his straw hat and laughs; the camera man chuckles aloud.

154

Dozens of ideas pop into my mind as I play; I play my parts each with a fresh enthusiasm, changing them, inventing, devising, accidentally producing unexpected effects, carefully working out others, enjoying every moment of it.

When the light falls in the evening I may sit a while, for coolness, in the basement set, where the glare of the reflectors has not beat all day. Then sometimes I think of the tricks fate has played with me since the days I clog-danced for Mr. Hawkins, and I wonder why and what the meaning of it all may be. But I never decide.

THE END

NOTES

Chapter 1

1. "Life itself . . . how you look at it." Cf. "Life is a tragedy when seen in close-up, but a comedy in long shot." —Chaplin quoted in *The Guardian* (London), December 29, 1977.

2. "My dream was to become a great musician." In *My Autobiography* (1964), hereinafter cited as *MA*, Chaplin mentions that the dawning of his musical consciousness occurred when, as a child, he heard "The Honeysuckle and the Bee" emanating from a pub at Kennington Cross in London. Harry C. Carr (*Photoplay*, July 1915, p. 28) quotes Chaplin thus: "Music, even in my poorhouse days, was always a passion with me. I never was able to take lessons of any kind, but I loved to hear music and could play any kind of instrument I could lay hands on." Actually, he played the piano, cello, and violin (all by ear), and because he was a southpaw, he had the strings on his cello and violin reversed so that he could play them with ease.

3. "an actor like Booth." Edwin [Thomas] Booth (1833–1893), the great American Shakespearean actor, brother of John Wilkes Booth, the assassin of Abraham Lincoln.

4. "Here I am . . . a millionaire." In 1916, the year *Charlie Chaplin's Own Story* (hereinafter cited as *CCOS*) was published, the comedian negotiated a contract with the Mutual Company that gave him $670,000 for making a dozen two-reelers. Three years earlier he had begun his film career by signing with Keystone at $150 per week.

5. "The public is like a child . . . throws them away." Cf. Chaplin's dialogue for *Limelight* (1952):

> CALVERO: I want to forget the public.
> TERRY: Never! You love them too much.
> CALVERO: I'm not so sure. Maybe I love them, but I don't admire them.
> TERRY: I think you do.
> CALVERO: As individuals—yes. There's greatness in everyone. But as a crowd they're like a monster without a head that never knows which way it's going to turn. . . .

6. "My mother . . . in an English hospital." Chaplin's mother was Hannah Chaplin née Hill, a music-hall performer who described herself as a "serio-comedienne, impersonator, and dancer" and went by

the stage name of Lily Harley. Chaplin's comment here was probably his first public announcement that his mother was still alive—but he took care not to explain the nature of her illness. In 1915, he told E. V. Whitcomb, an interviewer from *Photoplay*, that his mother was dead. In fact, around 1901 she had gone insane and was committed to Cane Hill asylum. She languished in Peckham House and other British mental institutions until 1921, when Chaplin sent his secretary, Tom Harrington, to bring her to the United States. Her mental condition at this time can be gauged from her response to the press on her arrival in New York. Asked, "Are you the mother of Charlie Chaplin?" she replied, "I'm the mother of Jesus Christ." Embarrassed by the revelation that his mother was mentally unbalanced, Chaplin explained to reporters that she had been shell-shocked in the recent European war! To the end of her days (she died in 1928 in the Santa Monica home that he had bought for her) Hannah never understood that her son had become a world celebrity.

The description here of Hannah as "one of the proudest, most gentle women in England," is typical of the extravagant claims that Chaplin made for her. He told Harry Carr (*Photoplay*, July 1915): "It seems to me that my mother was the most splendid woman I ever knew. I can remember how charming and well-mannered she was. She spoke four languages and had a good education. I have never met a more thoroughly refined woman than my mother." Unfortunately, it is rather hard to reconcile his statements with the impressions of reporters to whom she sounded like a Cockney barmaid, or with Chaplin's anecdote (*MA*, p. 57) in which Hannah calls a fellow-church-goer "Lady Shit." Would any refined Victorian/Edwardian lady have used such language?

7. "My father was a great, dark, handsome man." His real and stage name was Charles Chaplin. Like Hannah, Charlie's mother, he was a music-hall artiste; he sometimes referred to himself as a "topical vocalist." Hereafter he will be called Chaplin Sr.

In *MA*, p. 18, Chaplin states: "I was hardly aware of a father, and do not remember him having lived with us." However, in the same autobiography, he depicts this father of whom he was "hardly aware" as a faithless husband, an indifferent parent, a vicious bully, and a hopeless alcoholic, and in numerous vaudeville and movie portrayals, he held him up to ridicule in the character of the drunken dude or the big bully who terrorizes the Little Fellow. Chaplin's adoration of his mother (or at least of his fantasies about her) was, by contrast, the inspiration for his many distressed heroines who exist to be worshipped and defended by the Tramp. Doubts must linger as to whether Chaplin Sr. was as objectionable as his son paints him. But then objectivity is not to be expected in Oedipal relationships.

8. "I do not know my mother's real name. . . . music-hall actor."
Even within the context of *CCOS* one wonders how Chaplin could
have been certain that she came "of a good respected family in London" if he did not know her name. His comments here are totally
contradicted by *MA*, pp. 18-20, where we learn: (1) that his mother's
maiden name was Hannah Hill, (2) that she was the elder of two
daughters of an Irish cobbler named Charles Hill and his half-gypsy
wife, née Smith, (3) that at the age of eighteen she eloped with a
middle-aged man to Africa and had a child by him: Charlie's half-
brother Sydney, and (4) that on her return to England she married
Chaplin Sr. and had a child by him: Chaplin.

9. "They never made much money." This is contradicted little
more than a paragraph later when we are told that Chaplin Sr. "was a
great music-hall success." At that period, the golden age of British
music hall, successful performers were handsomely paid. Indeed, in
MA, p. 18, Chaplin informs us: "Even in those days he [Chaplin Sr.]
earned the considerable sum of forty pounds a week."

10. "Most of the time we lived very poorly." According to *MA* this
occurred later, when Chaplin's parents separated. Of the period while
they were still living together, *MA*, p. 14, notes: "Our circumstances
were moderately comfortable; we lived in three tastefully furnished
rooms."

11. "My brother Sydney." Actually Chaplin's half-brother. He was
born on March 17, 1885 in Cape Town, South Africa. Sydney helped
Chaplin land his most important vaudeville job—with the Karno Company. Later, he became Chaplin's business manager and also appeared
in several of his brother's First National pictures.

In *MA*, p. 19, Chaplin neatly sidesteps the identity of Sydney's
father by informing us that Hannah told her two sons that Sydney was
"the son of a lord." But biographer Gerith Von Ulm, deriving his information from Kono, Chaplin's Japanese secretary, chauffeur, and
confidant, had earlier identified Sydney's father as a Jewish book-
maker named Sydney Hawkes. Von Ulm also revealed that Hannah
had had another child, Wheeler, by a man named Dryden (see Von
Ulm, *Charlie Chaplin: King of Tragedy*, 1940, p. 31). Columnist Nora
Laing interviewed Wheeler in 1951. He told her that his father had
died twelve years earlier and that his name had been George Dryden.
Concerning Chaplin, he observed: "Our mother and my father separated, and Charlie and I never met again until I came to America in
1918. Charlie was already famous. We both agreed that it would be
better for me to make good on my own." (*Evening News*, London, December 13, 1951). Theodore Huff (*Charlie Chaplin*, 1952, p. 302) gives
Wheeler's birthyear as 1892, three years after Chaplin's. This suggests
that Chaplin's parents may have separated because Chaplin Sr. had

discovered that Hannah had been having an affair with George Dryden. It is significant that the Drydens are nowhere mentioned in either *CCOS* or *MA*. Chaplin obscured Sydney's paternity and suppressed any mention of Wheeler presumably in order to protect his mother's memory. However, he broke silence on the subject of Wheeler in *My Life in Pictures*, 1975, pp. 290–291. In connection with *Monsieur Verdoux*, he notes: "One of my assistant directors was Wheeler Dryden—who was in fact my half brother. His father, a well-known singer called Leo Dryden [sic], had seduced my mother and after their son was born had taken him away to live in Canada. . . . I found work for him [Wheeler] of various kinds in several of my films. He died in 1957." Hannah seems to have had fewer qualms than Chaplin about acknowledging her relationship with Wheeler. Chaplin notes (op. cit.), "I shall never forget Wheeler turning up in Hollywood after I became famous and while my mother was still alive. He made a very dramatic entrance and said: "Do you know who I am?" To which she calmly replied: "Of course I do. You're my son. Sit down and have a cup of tea."

12. "I was born in a little town in France." However, according to *MA*, p. 14, he was born "on April 16, 1889, at eight o'clock at night in East Lane, Walworth [London]."

In various articles and interviews during the teens, Chaplin claimed that he had been born in Fontainebleau near Paris. As his fame grew, various other cities and countries were quick to claim him for their own and Charlie did little or nothing to deny the rumors. Thus Leslie Goodwins observed: "It has been variously asserted that Chaplin is a Parisian, a Spaniard, a Mexican, and even an Argentine. . ." ("The Most Popular Man in the English-Speaking World," *The Landmark* I [September 1919] no. 2, p. 583). In the twenties when he paid his first triumphal return visit to England, he began admitting that he was a Londoner by birth. The Fontainebleau myth persisted, however, until it was finally scotched in 1927 by French biographer Edouard Ramond after he had checked the appropriate birth registers. "Charles Chaplin," he wrote, "était né, le 16 avril 1889, dans un faubourg de Londres! Oui, dans un faubourg de Londres, tout simplement ainsi que le doit un sujet de sa Majesté Britannique, et non pas à Fontainebleau, ainsi qu'on l'a prétendu. Charlie lui-même l'aurait déclaré—En êtes-vous sur? En tout cas l'auteur de ces lignes est certain que, ni à la date du 16 avril 1889, ni les jours qui suivent, les registres de l'état civil de Fontainebleau ne s'enrichirent d'une inscription qui les gonflerait d'orgueil aujourd'hui. Un titre de gloire de moins pour Fontainebleau, un de plus pour Londres" (*La Passion de Charlie Chaplin*, Paris: Librairie Baudinière [1927], p. 253). Thereafter, most biographers were convinced that Chaplin was a Londoner, but there was no agreement on exactly where in London he had been born. Columnist Jympson Harmon threw up his hands in despair at the start of a serialized biography of Chaplin: "I failed to find out where Charlie was born and I don't believe anyone else has fared better" (*Evening News*, London, September 9, 1952). John Montgomery noted: "He was born . . . if one is to believe a relative, at 287 Kennington Road, London. But according to author Thomas Burke [in his *City of Encounters*] he was born in Chester street, which runs between Kennington Road and Lower Kennington Lane" (*Comedy Films*, London: George Allen and Unwin, Ltd., 1954, p. 97). By contrast, Charlie's son, Charles Chaplin Jr., stated that his father was born at 3 Parnell Terrace, Kennington Road, which is almost certainly an error for 3 Pownall Terrace, an address at which Charlie lived for a time during his childhood, but where he was not actually born. On Chaplin's birthplace, see the Appendix.

13. "Lily Harley." Hannah may have chosen this stage name because it had echoes of Lily Langtry (1852–1929), the actress and beauty who became intimate with the Prince of Wales before he became Edward VII.

14. "she sang character songs." See program for one of her performances in *My Life in Pictures*, p. 43.

15. "Charles Chaplin, the singer of descriptive ballads." See the sheet-music covers displaying his performances in *My Life in Pictures*, pp. 44–45. Typically, Chaplin Sr. would saunter on stage dressed in a rakish top hat, a flamboyant cravat and natty morningsuit; one hand was in his pocket and the other would wave hail-fellow-well-met—as if to a street corner crony. He seems to have modelled his performances on those of George Leybourne, the original "Lion Comique" who, in the 1860s had roused British music-hall audiences with rollicking choruses of "Champagne Charlie". Chaplin Sr.'s tour-de-force was his song "Oui! Tray Bong! Or my Pal Jones" which he first rendered at the Old Gaiety in Birmingham and then at Seabright's in London where he received no less than six encores.

16. "We were at Aldershot." The town is located in Surrey; Sandhurst, the Royal Military College, is nearby.

17. "*Jack Jones.*" Chaplin provides the lyric in *MA*, p. 21.

Chapter 2

1. "I remember . . . that night." *MA*, pp. 20–21, gives a very different version of the "Jack Jones" anecdote. Chaplin tells us there that his performance at the canteen at Aldershot was his first appearance on stage; he was five years old. His parents had separated four years earlier and Chaplin Sr. was not present on that fateful evening. Chaplin was

standing in the wings when his mother's voice cracked and she was reduced to whispering. She fled from the stage amid a chorus of catcalls and the stage manager put little Charlie on in her place. He promptly launched into his rendering of "Jack Jones," a song associated with the popular Cockney comedian Gus Elen. Then, demonstrating more talent than sensitivity, he followed it up with an impersonation of his mother losing her voice. The delighted audience showered him with money, and when he announced that he wouldn't stop singing until he had picked up the coins, and then refused to allow the stage manager to help him collect the money, he received a tremendous ovation. This version of the anecdote is an unmistakable prototype of the Little Fellow rescuing a heroine in distress. It also presents Chaplin simultaneously usurping his mother's stage role (it was her last appearance on stage) and, more obliquely, his father's function as "breadwinner." For both acts he is rewarded and receives public acclaim. By contrast, the version in *CCOS* shows little Charlie being bullied by his drunken father into acting as his sick mother's savior. Chaplin Sr. is thus represented as the driving force that propelled Charlie into a theatrical career. *CCOS* also stresses that his parents quarrelled violently over whether or not he was too young to go on the stage; the implication is that it was Little Charlie's prodigious talents as much as his father's alcoholism that motivated his parents' separation. In both versions Chaplin is at pains to record that his first appearance on stage was also the turning point in the lives of one or both of his parents.

2. "He wanted to be a sailor." He did, in fact, become a naval cadet in Plymouth at the age of eleven, and at sixteen landed a job on a Donovan and Castle liner plying between England and South Africa (see R. J. Minney, *Chaplin the Immortal Tramp*, London, 1954, p. 9).

3. "So I came to be about ten years old. . . . clog dancers." He was eight, according to *MA*, p. 45, when Chaplin Sr. persuaded Hannah to *let him join* the clog-dancing troupe.

Clog dancing originated in Lancashire in the 1870s and became a popular British "folk art" by the end of the nineteenth century. It was a form of step dance in which the heels and toes beat out rapid and complex rhythms. The clogs used were not the quaint all-wooden Dutch variety but were made of leather uppers and wooden soles and heels equipped with metal tips and studs. See further Helen Frost, *Tap, Caper and Clog: Fifteen Character Dances*, 1931.

Chapter 3

1. "the five boys who had been clog dancing." Actually there were eight: the name of the troupe was the Eight Lancashire Lads.

2. "Mr. 'Awkins." See further G. J. Mellor, "The Making of Charlie

Chaplin," *Cinema Studies* II no. 2 (June 1966), pp. 19–25. Mellor's researches established that the manager of the troupe was a certain John Willie Jackson. *MA* also refers to him as Mr. Jackson.

According to Mellor, John Willie Jackson was a dour but kindly man, a devout Roman Catholic who loved children. He had five of his own and his attitude towards them was remarkably complaisant—except when he tempered gentleness with firmness in teaching them to dance. After his first wife died, he allowed his children to decide whether he should re-marry. When they encouraged him to do so, he found a second wife, as devout as himself, by advertising in the newspapers. Contrary to the account of him given in *CCOS* he does not seem to have been the sort of man from whom small boys fled in terror. He had not always been a professional dance-trainer. *MA*, p. 44, indicates that he had been a schoolteacher, but Mellor maintains that he had been a white-lead worker who merely taught clog dancing as a hobby until the white lead began to destroy his health. Then success in training his own children gave him the idea of launching them professionally. He formed them into a troupe in the summer of 1896. One of the eight "lads" was actually his daughter Rosie, whose hair was cut short to resemble a boy's. Jackson's four other children—John Willie Jr., Herbert, Alfred, and Stephen—were also members of the troupe, and three outsiders, George Cawley and his twin brothers Jim and Billy, were recruited to make up the full complement of eight. A few months of rigorous training enabled Jackson to transform these inexperienced youngsters into the best juvenile dancing troupe in England. When one of the Cawley boys became seriously ill, Mr. Holden, manager, of the Canterbury Theatre, recommended Chaplin as a replacement. On meeting the boy, Jackson immediately recognized him as a child he had seen dancing in the street to the strains of a barrel organ. *MA* indicates that it was Chaplin Sr. who came up with the idea of having the boy join a dance-troupe. Hannah, we are told, "was dubious at first until she met Mr. Jackson and his family, then she accepted."

The nature of Chaplin's remuneration differs according to source. *CCOS* mentions the sum of three shillings and sixpence per week as pocket money for Charlie plus a velvet suit and as much food as he could eat. *MA* mentions no allowance for Chaplin but merely board and lodging and half-a-crown a week for Hannah. Mellor states: "The 'Lads' got one pound each per week and their keep. . . ." For the 1890s this last amount sounds excessively generous—particularly for a novice like Chaplin.

As Chaplin was untrained as a clog dancer, Jackson spent six weeks teaching him the basic steps—hour upon hour of agonizing practice until at last he was ready to appear with the troupe. "At the end of the day he would often steal away into a corner behind some scenery and cry his baby heart out" (Leslie Goodwins, "The Most Popular Man in the

English-Speaking World," *The Landmark*, September 1919, p. 583). He had also lost the self-confidence he had demonstrated when standing in for his mother at the Aldershot Canteen. In *MA* he confesses: "confronting an audience . . . [now] gave me stage fright. I could hardly move my legs. It was weeks before I could solo dance as the rest of them did."

3. "It was a cold foggy night. . . ." The chronicle of suffering that follows and continues through chapter 5 differs totally from the account of Chaplin's experiences with the troupe as narrated in *MA*, ch. 3. The obvious source of the version in *CCOS* is Chaplin's recollection of *Oliver Twist* and *Nicholas Nickleby* rather than his actual childhood experiences.

The *CCOS* account can be interpreted as a fantasy of Chaplin's separation from his mother, the revelation of a "trauma" that is suppressed in *MA*. By referring to Mr. Jackson as "Hawkins," Chaplin conflates the names of Hawkes (see ch. 1, n. 11) and Chaplin Sr., thus uniting in one personage the identities of Chaplin's various "rivals" for the affections of Hannah: i.e., his mother's lover(s), his half-brother Sydney (whose surname should have been Hawkes), and his father. Hawkins, like Chaplin Sr., is represented as a bully who entices little Charlie away from his mother and forces him to perform for the amusement of a drunken rabble. The allusion to the "Lunnon" clog dance is an oblique relocation of the fantasy to a place where the traumatic separation occurred. The boy's flight from Hawkins brings him up against a cow (a rather obvious symbol for a docile, ineffective mother) and an aggressive dog (a "guardian" turned hostile) that drives him away from food and shelter. When, at last, he reaches Covent Garden, he starves in the midst of plenty until his mother providentially rescues him. All other adults are callously indifferent to his fate. Finally, back home, mother and son celebrate their reunion: an event that pointedly coincides with the fact that Charlie has Hannah all to himself. The nightmare of separation thus ends happily with a dream of wish-fulfillment.

4. "Hingratitude. . . . I won't 'ave it!" The dialogue is Dickensian rather than authentic-sounding Cockney, and Hawkins' comment about Charlie having a good kind master "wot never canes yer" recalls not only Mr. Squeers but also Mrs. Gargery who boasts of having brought up Pip "by hand."

Chapter 4

1. "Coom, coom. . ." The girl's dialect starts out as North-of-England then switches to Scots with "She wilna be vexed wi' a girt boy. . . ."

2. "girt" = great. The girl would probably have said "bairn" rather than "baaby."

3. "Barnet." North of London; as the crow flies, about twenty miles from Lambeth where the Chaplins lived.

Chapter 5

1. "brandysnaps" = wafer-like gingerbread.
2. "Lawk a mussy" = Lord have mercy.
3. "Covent Garden market." The place where 'Enry 'Iggins would one day meet Colonel Pickering also has Dickensian associations with Mr. Pickwick.
4. "a hokey-pokey man." A street vendor of candies. Hokey-pokey was actually a kind of English ice cream that was firmer than Italian ice cream. Vendors would pass through the streets of London calling out, "Hokey-pokey, penny a lump!" It has been suggested (*OED* and elsewhere) that the term arose as a corruption of the Italian *O che poco* = Oh, how little!

Chapter 6

1. "But most of all she taught me acting. . . . streets." Cf. Chaplin's description of his mother's acting in *MA*, pp. 23–24, and note also p. 68, where he observes: "Mother . . . would read to me or we would sit together at the window and she would amuse me by making remarks about the pedestrians as they passed by. She would invent stories about them. . . ." In his article, "What People Laugh At," *American Magazine*, November 1918, Chaplin states: "If it had not been for my mother . . . I doubt if I could have made a success of pantomime. She was one of the greatest pantomime artists I have ever seen. She would sit for hours at a window, looking down at the people on the street and illustrating with her hands, eyes, and facial expression just what was going on below. All the time she would deliver a running fire of comment. And it was through watching and listening to her that I learned not only how to express emotions with my hands and face, but also how to observe and study people. . . . This habit of studying people was the most valuable thing my mother could have taught me because it has been only this way that I have learned what appeals to human beings as funny."

Chapter 7

1. "a sovereign." This was a British gold coin approximately the size of a quarter and worth one pound sterling.
2. "My father had died suddenly the night before." Charles Chaplin Sr. died (of cirrhosis of the liver) at St. Thomas's Hospital, London on May 10, 1901. The allusion to his death in *CCOS* differs sharply from the account in *MA*, p. 58, where Chaplin describes vividly his last encounter with his father a few weeks before the latter's death. Both of these accounts differ from another of Chaplin's recollections quoted by R. J. Minney (*Chaplin—The Immortal Tramp*, London, 1954, p. 5): "I was only a

little kid at the time, but I can never forget that night [when he died] . . . I stood under the window . . . in the cold and darkness, sobbing my heart out waiting for the news I dreaded to hear." Denis Gifford, *The Movie Makers: Chaplin*, New York, 1974, p. 14, reprints Chaplin Sr.'s brief obituary notice in *Era*.

3. "the funeral." See the different and far more detailed account in *MA*, pp. 58–59. See also Raoul Sobel & David Francis, *Chaplin: Genesis of a Clown*, London, 1977, p. 62.

4. "I put my hands in my pockets . . . went out into the street." *MA*, ch. 4, is far more informative on the events following Chaplin Sr.'s death and Hannah's hospitalization.

Chapter 8

1. "I was only one of thousands as wretched as I." For a firsthand account of poverty in London at this period see Jack London's *People of the Abyss* (1903).

2. "He was much interested in hearing. . . . He had never had a mother." There is suggestion here of Barrie's *Peter Pan*. As a child Chaplin may have played a wolf in a revival of Barrie's play about the motherless boy who would not grow up. See the introduction, n. 24.

3. "His name was Snooper . . . rents in his coat." This creation is unmistakably modeled on John Dawkings, the Artful Dodger in *Oliver Twist*.

4. "glom the leather" = snatch the purse. "Glom" is probably a corruption of "glim" from "glim-jack"—thieves' cant for a sneak-thief or a thief who operates under cover of night.

Chapter 9

1. "I am coming back from Africa." At the age of 16 Sydney had become a bugler on a Donovan and Castle liner plying between England and South Africa. See *MA*, pp. 62, 67.

Chapter 10

1. "a Norfolk suit" = a two-piece suit with a belted jacket that has box pleats at front and back. (A Norfolk jacket and knicker-bockers were frequently worn by Bernard Shaw.)

Chapter 11

1. *"From Rags to Riches."* A play by Charles A. Taylor. See the Introduction, p. xv.

2. "what's the screw?" = "What's the wages?"

Chapter 12

1. "Burton Crescent." Probably Burton Grove, Walworth, in South London.
2. "Sweetbay." Not located in any gazetteer of the British Isles consulted by the present editor.

Chapter 13

1. *"Floats"*—a theatrical trade paper.

Chapter 14

1. "it was not easy to get a hearing on the Strand"—i.e., to get assistance from the London theatrical agents, many of whose offices were located in The Strand, a thoroughfare just north of the Thames.
2. "the cold pasty." A British variety of meat pie covered with a crust.
3. The finale of this chapter anticipates Calvero's visit to his agent in *Limelight*.

Chapter 15

1. *"Jim, the Romance of a Cockney."* A play by H. A. Saintsbury, correctly titled *Jim: A Romance of Cockayne*. See the Introduction, p. xvi
2. *"Sherlock Holmes."* William Gillette's dramatization of the stories by Conan Doyle. See the Introduction, p. xvii.
3. "William Gillette." Celebrated American actor and dramatist (1855–1937), particularly memorable for his string of successes as the star of his own melodramas, some of which were adapted from popular fiction.
4. "Charles Frohman." The great American actor-manager (1860–1915) who controlled some of the most important theaters in New York and London.

Chapter 16

1. "a Japanese servant." Later, when he became affluent, Chaplin acquired a Japanese general factotum named Kono—see ch. 1, n. 11, and *MA*, pp. 371–373.
2. "Billy." Chaplin played this role in both the 1903 revival of *Sherlock Holmes* and in Gillette's brief skit, *The Painful Predicament of Sherlock Holmes* (1905). The character, originally created by Henry McArdle in the 1901 production of *Sherlock Holmes*, was that of a quick-witted page-boy. See the Introduction, p. xix.

3. "Mr. Postham." His name seems to have been William Postance, but Chaplin refers to him as Postant in *MA*, pp. 88–89, and in *Limelight*—where he is played by the avuncular Nigel Bruce as an impresario rather than a stage manager.

4. "*Clarice*." A comedy by Gillette in which he co-starred with Lucille La Verne and Marie Doro. See the Introduction, p. xx.

Chapter 17

1. "Prince Christian." Probably the Crown Prince of Denmark who became King Christian X (reigned 1912–1947).

2. "A sudden chuckle from King Edward." The British sovereign Edward VII had an unpredictable and explosive sense of humor. While watching Bernard Shaw's play *John Bull's Other Island* (1904), he laughed so violently that the seat under him collapsed.

3. "Mrs. Kendal." Madge [Margaret] Kendal née Robertson (1848–1935), sister of the dramatist T. W. Robertson and wife of British actor-manager William Hunter Kendal (1843–1917). Madge Kendal was one of the great actresses of her generation and was particularly brilliant at comedy.

Chapter 18

1. "Irene Vanbrugh." Like Madge Kendal, Irene Vanbrugh (1872–1949) was an outstanding comedienne, renowned for her scintillating performances in plays by Oscar Wilde, Pinero, and Barrie.

Chapter 19

1. "*The Strand*." The celebrated British magazine in which many of Conan Doyle's *Sherlock Holmes* stories were first published.

2. "cutting a dash" = being notable, making a display.

Chapter 20

1. "the North End of London." A Londoner would be more likely to say *the North of London* or *North London*.

Chapter 21

1. "an Irish bull." An expression containing a ludicrous inconsistency or an obvious contradiction in terms. (There was once a folk belief that live Irish bulls flourished if slices of meat were cut from them.)

2. "*Casey's Circus*." See the Introduction, p. xxiii.

Chapter 22

1. "Doctor Body"—a parody of 'Dr.' Bodie. See the Introduction, p. xxiv.

2. "Karno." Fred Karno (1886–1941), the comedy king of the late Victorian and Edwardian music-halls. See the Introduction, p. xxvi.

Chapter 23

1. "the Keith circuit . . . The Orpheum circuit." Chains of vaudeville theaters. The first was controlled by Benjamin Franklin Keith and Edward Franklin Albee; by 1920 it embraced more than 400 theaters in the eastern half of the United States. Martin Beck's smaller circuit extended west of Chicago to the Pacific coast.

Chaplin's first U.S. vaudeville tour (1911) was actually on the Sullivan and Considine theater circuit which involved playing in several Canadian cities as well as coast to coast in the United States. He played the Keith-Albee circuit on his second tour (1912–13).

Chapter 24

1. "Mr. Reeves, the manager of the American company." Alfred Reeves (1866–1946) was a circus manager before joining the Karno Company. In 1918 he became Chaplin's general manager and vice-president of the Chaplin Film Corp.

2. "Marcus Loew, a New York theatrical producer." (1870–1927). He also created Metro-Goldwyn-Mayer.

3. "*A Night in a London Music-Hall.*" Correctly called *A Night in an English Music Hall*, the American title of the Karno skit *Mumming Birds* which, in its first production (1904), starred Billie Ritchie as the drunken swell (Chaplin's role) and Charley Bell as the bad lad in the theater-box. In 1915 Chaplin re-created the skit as a film, *A Night in the Show*, playing two roles: Mr. Pest, a drunken swell in the orchestra, and Mr. Rowdy, a drunken tramp in the gallery. See the Introduction, p. xxxvi.

4. "Mack Sennett." Born Michael Sinnott (1880–1960), production head of the Keystone Film Company; known as the King of [Slapstick] Comedy. See Kalton Lahue, *Mack Sennett's Keystone* (1971) and Kalton Lahue and Terry Brewer, *Kops and Custards* (1968).

5. "Twelve months later . . . When can you start?" There are many different stories about how Chaplin came to be hired by the Keystone Company. Chaplin himself is quite inconsistent about how it happened (cf. *CCOS* with *MA*, p. 138), while Mack Sennett recalls things quite differently from Chaplin (see Mack Sennett, *King of Comedy*, 1954, chapter 14). No one seems to agree—even on the amount Chaplin received for his first movie contract.

Chapter 25

1. "a snare-drum" = a small, two-headed drum carried at the side and with a metal or catgut strings stretched across each drumhead.
2. "Keystone studios." They were located in Edendale.

Chapter 26

1. "You're a hungry tramp in the country." What follows in this chapter and the next provides the only account of two rejected Chaplin films made before his first released movie, *Making a Living*. Although there is no evidence to support this account, we should remember that *CCOS* was published close in time to the events of these chapters (i.e., some three years later), so that Chaplin might well have been cautious not to publish facts that could easily have been contradicted by people from Keystone. On the other hand, perhaps with deliberate circumspection, these chapters nowhere mention Chaplin's famous quarrel with director Henry Lehrman over the first Chaplin picture (see *MA*, pp. 143–144) or even Lehrman's name. One of their objectives is clearly to establish the impression that after two brief abortive efforts Chaplin became an instant success by taking over the direction of his own movies. This was not in fact the case. See further chs. 28, n. 1, and 29, nn. 1 and 2.

Chapter 28

1. "My cane . . . on the stage." Chapter 26 conveys the information that Chaplin's (unnamed) director assigned the comedian to play the role of a tramp; this chapter indicates that it was Chaplin himself who came up with the idea of the famous costume. *MA* and other sources contradict these notions. Thus *MA*, p. 45, mentions that at the age of eight Chaplin dreamed of appearing in a music hall act consisting of "two boys dressed as comedy tramps . . . but, alas, it never materialized." At that period tramp acts were not uncommon on the music hall circuits that Chaplin toured with the Eight Lancashire Lads, and one such act that he recollected having tried unsuccessfully to imitate was Zarmo "the comedy tramp juggler" (*MA*, p. 47). Presumably, like so many comedians, Chaplin was also influenced by the great Dan Leno, who frequently appeared on stage wearing absurdly elongated boots and oversized pants that flapped loosely around his frail limbs. It should also be noted that in 1906 when Chaplin joined the company of *Casey's Circus*, he appeared with a cast of juveniles who wore clothes that were many sizes too big for them and who burlesqued the behavior of adults. Charles Chaplin Jr., in his book *My Father, Charlie Chaplin* (1960), states with seeming authority: ". . . My father told me once that the costume had really originated years before. One night when he was janitoring in a London music hall, the

frantic manager came to him with the dismal news that the star comedian was sick and he needed a fill-in. Would Dad help out? The comedian was a big man and his clothes were oversize for Dad—the pants baggy, the shoes too large. But the derby was small, because Dad's head was larger than the comedian's. 'I just put them on and there was my tramp outfit,' my father told me. . . ." Two details of this story cast doubt on its reliability. First, there is no evidence that Chaplin ever worked as a janitor in a music hall; second, it sounds highly unlikely that the manager of a music hall would ask a mere janitor to stand in for the star comedian. However, this anecdote does lend some support to the probability that the tramp role and costume originated earlier than Chaplin's start with Keystone. Nevertheless, tradition has it that Chaplin assembled the costume for the first time by borrowing a pair of Fatty Arbuckle's pants, Ford Sterling's oversize boots (put on the wrong feet), a small derby hat that belonged to Minta Durfee's father, and one of Mack Swain's moustaches trimmed into a rectangular shape.

Chapter 29

1. "When my first comedy . . . *Laughing Gas*." Chaplin's first comedy for Keystone was *Making a Living*, which premiered on February 2, 1914. *Caught in the Rain* (May 4, 1914) was his thirteenth and *Laughing Gas* (July 9, 1914) was his twentieth comedy for Keystone. The first script Chaplin wrote for a movie appears to have been his eleventh Keystone, *Twenty Minutes of Love* (April 20, 1914). He codirected his next film, *Caught in a Cabaret* (April 27, 1914), with Mabel Normand. His first film as solo director was evidently *Caught in the Rain* (May 4, 1914). The tramp character originally appeared in the Keystone film, *Kid Auto Races at Venice* (February 7, 1914). He reappeared in many but not all of the 33 subsequent Keystones.

2. "*Dough and Dynamite*." Chaplin's twenty-ninth Keystone, released August 26, 1914.

3. "Keep your eye piped." Addressing his ex-sailor brother, Chaplin uses an appropriately nautical term which once signified *weep*; here it means *keep your eyes peeled*.

Chapter 30

1. "a thousand little figures of Charlie Chaplin." See the souvenir items depicted in Gerald McDonald's *The Picture History of Charlie Chaplin* (1965) and *Chaplin's My Life in Pictures* (1975). In *MA* p. 173, Chaplin, writing about his experiences in 1915, observes: "Although I knew the extent of my success in Los Angeles by the long lines at the box office, I did not realize to what magnitude it had grown elsewhere. In New York, toys and statuettes of my character were being sold in all the department

stores and drugstores. Ziegfeld Follies girls were doing Chaplin numbers, marring their beauty with mustaches, derby hats, and baggy trousers, singing a song called 'Those Charlie Chaplin Feet.' " We were also inundated with all manner of business propositions involving books, clothes, candles, toys, cigarettes, and toothpaste." The Essanay Company, for whom Chaplin was working at this period, became actively involved in the marketing of Chaplin souvenirs—as evidenced in their promotion of *The Charlie Fun Book* and the *Charlie Chaplin Scream Book* which contained extensive advertising for the Essanay comedies.

Chapter 31

1. "The situation . . . I called in Sydney." *MA*, p. 173, notes: "My success had taken on such proportions that Sydney now intended devoting his whole time to my business affairs." Previously Sydney had appeared in his own, less successful series of Keystone comedies playing a character named Gussie, and in the featurette *A Submarine Pirate*. Chaplin later gave him memorable supporting character roles in *A Dog's Life, Shoulder Arms, Pay Day,* and *The Pilgrim.* Thereafter his most notable screen appearance was as Old Bill in the Vitaphone movie *The Better 'Ole* (1926).

2. "the offer of the Essanay company . . . my films." *MA* tells us that G. M. Anderson, copartner with George K. Spoor of the Essanay Company, agreed to Chaplin's demand of $1250 per week and a $10,000 bonus (p. 160); seven pages later Chaplin refers to the weekly salary as $1200. In the same work (p. 159) Chaplin informs us that he decided to quit Keystone because Sennett refused to pay him $1,000 per week.

3. "Hutchinson of the Mutual." Chaplin's contract with Essanay expired at the end of 1915 and he signed up with the Mutual Film Corporation on February 26, 1916. Initial negotiations towards the Mutual contract were conducted by Charles Hutchinson for Mutual and Sydney Chaplin on behalf of his brother. Hutchinson was President of the American Film Manufacturing Company whose movies were released under the Mutual logo. *Moving Picture World* for March 11, 1916 noted: "Charles Chaplin, not yet twenty-seven years old . . . signed an agreement to play for one year in pictures to be released on the Mutual program. He will direct his own subjects and will make two reels each month. A company has been formed to take charge of the Chaplin productions. This company will pay Chaplin a salary of $10,000 a week. For signing the contract the comedian was given a bonus of $150,000. Which means, of course, $520,000 plus $150,000—$670,000. It would seem that never in the history of the stage and its related arts has there been a salary of this magnitude. What makes the story doubly interesting is the fact that in the figures named there is every reason to believe the

usual rather than the unusual multiplication of the actuality has been omitted."

4. "Mr. Caulfield." Henry P. Caulfield, manager of the company formed to take charge of the Chaplin productions that were to be released under the Mutual logo.

5. "Mr. Freuler." John R. Freuler who signed the Mutual contract. A movie record of this event is still extant, and a clip from it appears in the Chaplin biography film, *The Gentleman-Tramp*.

Chapter 32

1. "the Lone Star company." An ad in *The Motion Picture News* described the new studio thus: "Situate on the fringe of the motion picture studio area in Hollywood, it occupies a whole block and is probably the most pleasant studio in California."

2. "She cannot come to America . . . sea trip." She survived it easily enough in 1921: see ch. 1, n. 6.

Chapter 33

1. "the chauffeur." He was Kono, Chaplin's Japanese factotum. He drove Chaplin's first car, a seven-passenger Locomobile "which in those days was considered the best car in America." Chaplin paid $4,900 for it. See *MA*, p. 189.

APPENDIX
Chaplin's Birthplace

At the opening of the first chapter of *My Autobiography* Chaplin states categorically, "I was born on April 16, 1889, at eight o'clock at night in East Lane, Walworth." Like so many of his pronouncements about his childhood this one is unverifiable and open to serious question.

It is impossible to establish his actual date of birth because his birth was not registered at Somerset House as British law required. Thus Chaplin's claim, in *My Autobiography*, to have been his mother's only *legitimate* offspring is highly dubious. One is left wondering whether his motive in making such a claim was either to camouflage his mother's questionable reputation or to affirm his own "respectability." Or perhaps both?

It is equally impossible to prove that he was born in East Lane, Walworth. *My Autobiography* informs us that Charles Hill, Chaplin's maternal grandfather, established himself in a boot-repairing business in East Lane. From this tidbit, Walworth's local history concludes that the comedian was born "in a room over his grandfather's boot-repairer's shop."[1] Charlie *may* have been born in East Lane, but not necessarily in or over his grandfather's shop—if, indeed, his grandfather had a shop. *Kelly's Post Office London Directory* for 1889 lists fourteen boot and shoe repairers in East Lane—but not one was named Charles Hill and the name Charles Hill does not appear on the local electoral register for that year. The only Hill in residence in East Lane during 1889 was George Hill, a shirt and collar dresser living at no. 237. It is possible, of course, that Grandpa Hill did not own his own shop, that he managed or worked in someone else's establishment—in which case his name would not have appeared in the *Directory*.

Apropos of East Lane itself, a letter of January 13, 1977, from M. K. A. Doughty (Borough Librarian and Curator for Southwark) to the present writer states: "East Street . . . has always been and still is referred to by residents of Walworth as either 'East Lane' or just 'The Lane,' and in fact, on a map of 1860, part of the street is labelled East Street and part East Lane. However, by 1870, on an Ordnance Survey map of that year it is called East Street." In 1889 the Walworth Road end of East Lane was (as it still is) a street market. A spectrum of shops lined each side of the narrow street. In front of these shops were (and are) a crowded array of stalls offering a variety of provisions. East Lane has always been a hive of activity, but the busiest places (when Chaplin was growing up there) were Telling's the pawnbroker, the stewed eel and fried fish shops, and the four pubs scattered at convenient intervals along the north side of the street. There were no pubs at the Old Kent Road end of East Lane: that section had the reputation of being more "upper class."

The present writer visited the area in October 1977 and discovered that the Old Kent Road end of East Lane retains vestiges of the character it possessed in the eighteen-nineties: there is still a fish-and-chip shop located among the once proud homes of artisans and more affluent workers, and a row of the old bollards to which cabbies used to tether their horses continues to sprout rather pointlessly out of the pavement. Except for the East Street Baptist Church (originally the Richmond Street Mission) the middle section of East Lane is entirely transformed: the Blitz destroyed most of the old shops and a new housing development has taken their place. The market area, at the Walworth Road end, has undoubtedly diminished in size, and the market itself, specializing mainly in fish, fruit, and vegetables, is far less colorful than it used to be when, before World War II, shoppers were regularly cajoled by racing tipsters and street entertainers, by hucksters pushing patent medicines, and by hawkers touting everything from cut flowers to secondhand bicycles. To all intents and purposes it was a smaller version of Petticoat Lane Market.

It should be noted that one aged local resident of Walworth maintained that Chaplin was born "in some tenement flats" at the Walworth Road end of East Lane.[2] If this is correct then Chaplin was probably born in Manchester Buildings—now Peabody Buildings—between 15 and 17 East Lane. It is noteworthy that no. 15 was the shop of a boot and shoe maker called Nathaniel Harris.

NOTES

1. Anon., *The Story of Walworth* (London: Borough of Southwark Neighbourhood Histories no. 4., 1976), p. 17. See also E. J. Orford ed., *The Book of Walworth* (London: Browning Hall, 1925).

2. J. H. Bennett, *I Was a Walworth Boy*, unpublished ms. on file in Newington Butt's Library. Bennett was born in East Lane in 1902 and his memoir gives a detailed description of the "Lane" c. 1910–1914.